HARRY FERGUSON:
BEFORE THE PLOUGH

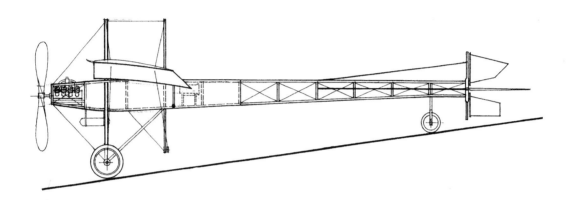

by Michael Clarke
in collaboration with Jack Woods

BALLYHAY BOOKS

First published by Ballyhay Books,
an imprint of Laurel Cottage Ltd.
Ballyhay, Donaghadee, N. Ireland 2009.
Copyrights Reserved.
© Text Michael Clarke and Jack Woods 2009.
All rights reserved.
No part of this book may be reproduced or stored on any media
without the express written permission of the publishers.
Design & origination in N. Ireland.
Printed by Gutenberg Press Ltd., Malta.
ISBN 978 1 900935 81 4

The photographs on the following pages are reproduced courtesy of the Ferguson Family
Museum, Freshwater, Isle of Wight: pp 7, 8,9,17, 32, 48, 53, 54, 70, 73, 74, 78, 79, 80, 89,
90, 91, 107, 108, 109, 110, 111, 114, 117, 118, 119, 125
We gratefully acknowledge the following for contributing their photographs: Irish Motor
News (pages 13, 25, 62, 81, 82), Michael Clarke (143, 145, 148, 149, 150), B. Blaney/S.
Christie (23, 24, 26, 27), Leeds University (63, 120, 121, 130), Rhoda Cinnamond (100,
104, 133), Jack Woods (38, 153), Royal Aeronautical Society (55, 56), Henry V Bell (18),
Short Bros (37), Belfast Evening Telegraph (46), Public Records Office of Northern Ireland
(47), Belfast Telegraph (50), Point Bar (69), Ireland's Saturday Night (77), Norman Kerr
(112), Beaulieu Motor Museum (116), Royal Aero Club (132)

Contents

Acknowledgements

It has been a great pleasure working with Michael Clarke on the production of this book. Without his input you would not have had such a detailed and informative record about Harry Ferguson's career before the plough. Therefore I must take this opportunity to thank Michael most sincerely for agreeing to write the book. With his talents, and my good looks, we formed a formidable team.

Michael has brought to this book his enthusiasm and knowledge of the pioneer days of aviation, his skill as an architect – as shown in the detailed line drawings – as well as his finesse and attention to detailed writing. I would like to thank Michael not only for these skills but for his friendship, gracious attitude and wit. I must also thank Muriel, his wife, who always had a welcome and some culinary delights each time I visited their home.

Thanks and appreciation also go – in no particular order – to:

Belfast Central Library, in particular Yvonne Lynn; Charlotte Murtagh; Rhoda Cinnamond, Public Records Office Northern Ireland; Ian Montgomery, National Library of Ireland Dublin, Shorts Tec. Library, Special Collections Leeds University, Peter Warr, curator of the Ferguson Family Museum.

Jack Woods

Author's Note

Harry Ferguson: Before the Plough is the result of an idea formulated by my friend Jack Woods, and would not, and could not, have happened without him.

Jack, who has a comprehensive knowledge of aviation generally and a particular interest in the history of aviation in Ireland, realised that the centenary of Harry Ferguson's first flight would occur in December 2009, and considered that something should be done to recognise this event. He also realised that although Harry Ferguson's life has been well documented, much of the emphasis had quite rightly been placed on his agricultural achievements, while his early prowess in motorsports and his considerable aeronautical work has been less well covered. Jack put these two considerations together and came up with the idea for this book. He enthusiastically encouraged me, using guile and flattery, to take on the task and, being half way there as a fellow enthusiast, I agreed to have a go, but only if he could do the basic research – I would, if he could!

He has kept his part of the bargain and has produced information and photos from all sorts of sources, to the extent that I could hardly keep up and, when I flagged, his enthusiasm and encouragement kept me going.

It has been a pleasure working with Jack on this project, and I hope that the result of our cooperation will go some way to fill a gap in the knowledge and understanding of this period in Harry Ferguson's eventful life.

My primary thanks go to my wife, Muriel, for her patience during the neglectful periods of writing and putting together the text, and while accompanying me during excursions to obscure locations in search of information, and to absorb atmosphere.

Her help in reading over the script, identifying errors in grammar, spacing, punctuation etc., and in making positive suggestions on the sense of the text has been vital, although I reserve the right to be blamed for any and all such elements as printed! Thanks are also due to my son Ian, who got me out of the all too many glitches that my geriatric, one-fingered word-processing created.

A great many others have helped in all sorts of ways, patiently and freely answering questions, providing information, making suggestions, or simply contributing their encouragement. I list below, in no special order, the names of as many of these helpers as I can remember with my sincere thanks, and apologise to those I may have missed out;

Brian Macdonald, Hugh McGrattan, Jim Hamilton, Mary Hamilton, William Kyle, Rhoda Cinnamond, William Ellames, Victor O'Hara, Paul Wilkinson, Harry Peden, Rev. G. Glasgow, William Morrison, Jennifer Cunningham, Hugh Leeke, George Thompson, David Gilliland, Robert T. Killen, Liam Kelly, Robert Guthrie, Ken Ferris, Maurice Patton, Jimmy Gilliland, Robert Ballagh and Trevor Taylor.

My thanks also go to the Ulster Folk and Transport Museum for allowing me complete access to the fine full-size replica of the Ferguson Mark 2 they have on display.

Michael Clarke

In the Beginning

James and Mary Ferguson pose with a friend in front of Lake House, Growell

On November 4th 1884 a son was born to James and Mary Ferguson at Lake House, Growell in County Down, Northern Ireland. He was the fourth of eleven children, three girls and eight boys. The family lived on their 100 acre farm in drumlin country beside Lough Aghery, between Hillsborough and Dromara.

Nothing unusual about any of that you might think. Large families were the norm in those days and were especially useful on a farm where there were always chores to be done, even by children, and in any case infant mortality was an ever present danger, while family planning was still in the future.

But this particular boy was a bit special. In the future he would make a very significant impact on life all over the world, directly and indirectly. He was christened Henry George but never received anything other than Harry.

His father, James Ferguson, came from a line of Scottish Fergusons who had settled in the Dromara area some 200 years earlier. His present 100 acre holding gave a reasonable prosperity for the time, although it entailed long hours of hard work 6 days a week and required careful husbanding of the acreage and of the animals, and keen trading in the markets. There was little time on the farm for relaxation or amusements and the latter were significantly missing in their family way of life.

James was a naturally austere man and a strict head of family. He was deeply religious and belonged to the Plymouth Brethren, a Christian sect that had broken away from the Anglican Church some sixty years earlier. They believed in the literal interpretation of the Bible, preached the Second Coming of Christ and dispensed with an ordained, salaried clergy.

Initially the Brethren held their meetings in members' homes around the country, with local lay preachers leading their devotions. When the local congregation around Growell grew in strength James donated a nearby piece of his land for the erection of a Mission Hall which stands to this day.

This photograph of James Ferguson seems to portray the serious-minded man that he certainly was – even on a day at the seaside! In fairness, cameras of the day required the subject to sit still and be composed

At Lake House a strict observance of Bible teachings was imposed on all aspects of family life and when travelling lay preachers visited Growell they would stay with the Fergusons, involving the family in further extensive Bible readings and prayer sessions.

So life on the Lake House farm was quite stiff and restricting, particularly on the natural exuberance of the children, already subject to the then normal Victorian attitude that children are to be seen and not heard, while the expectation and need for even the youngest to play their part in the working of the farm further pressurised their early years.

Slight relief from these day-to-day pressures came from the milder, gentler nature of their mother Mary. Mary came from a more open family background. Although also belonging to the Brethren, her father Graham Bell had a more relaxed nature and held quite enlightened views for that time, exemplified by the encouragement of his two daughters by a second marriage to become doctors, a considerable rarity in those

Harry's mother having a relaxing moment in Lake House at Growell

days. Visits by the Ferguson children to the lively Bell household in Newry were great treats and clearly a wonderful contrast to life at home.

This rather rigid lifestyle at Lake House did nevertheless have some positive and practical effects on the children's development. Their self discipline, their application to the task in hand and their attitude to tidiness and precision all show up later on, none more so than the approach of Harry and his older brother Joe to their later business enterprises.

Such was the atmosphere in which Harry grew up, but as has already been alluded to he was a bit special and, from quite an early age, Harry displayed an independence of thought and action that cut across the grain of this regime, leading to minor altercations in his early years and to more serious disagreements later on, as he developed a greater certainty and confidence in himself.

A small example of early spirit is recounted about an occasion on the farm when, at the age of four, an approaching farm worker wishing to get past him with a heavy wheelbarrow called out,

"Harry, you're in my way!", only to be rebuffed with, "No, you're in Harry's way!"

There were two National Schools, Drumlough and Ballykeel, near Lake House at that time. Although Ballykeel was just over ¾ mile from home and Drumlough was twice that distance, it was to the Drumlough school that the Ferguson children were sent, and over the twenty year period between 1885 and 1905 there was at least one Ferguson child in attendance there. See Appendix 1 for details of the Ferguson family.

At the age of 4 years and 4 months, on 5th March 1889, Harry was enrolled at Drumlough, and for the next ten years or so made the daily 1½ mile journeys to and from school on foot, come rain or shine. As far as is known his school days seem to have been largely uneventful, but towards the end of his time there another indication of independence and early confidence occurred. Following an incident in class he felt that a fellow pupil had been wrongfully chastised for a misdemeanour that he had not committed and argued so strongly with the principal that he had to be taken away from school. The records of Drumlough School show a period of 7 months when, between being struck off on 15th October 1898 and being re-admitted on 16th May 1899, he was clearly not at Drumlough. Jim Hamilton of Hillsborough Road, near Ballykeel recalls his father telling him that Harry had attended the Ballykeel school where he too had been educated, so it would seem that Harry was at Ballykeel during the period in question. The Ballykeel school was eventually closed, becoming a residence for a time before it was finally demolished and replaced by a modern dwelling.

In recounting the above episode it is interesting to relate an account of a rather similar one involving Harry's older brother Joe who also attended the Drumlough school, starting four years before Harry. Hugh Watson, later Rev. Watson, who had been a monitor to Master Whiteside at the school when the brothers were there, recalled how two young children who were neighbours of the Fergusons arrived late for school. As they entered the school yard they feared what punishment might be in store for them, panicked, and turned for home. But they had been seen by Mr Whiteside and he sent the monitor out to fetch them back. They were brought up in front of the class and the master was seen to reach for his cane. Joe, sitting in the front row, realised what was about to happen and, without a moment's hesitation, sprang up between the cowering children and the master and, offering out his hand, said, "I will take their punishment." Mr Whiteside immediately relented at this gesture and set aside his cane. These two episodes leave a clear impression of two boys with inherent feelings for fairness and directness, qualities that would be beneficial in later life, while the actions themselves would be well remembered by fellow pupils and become part of the Ferguson reputation for robust and honest dealing.

Harry finally left Drumlough National School on 23rd December 1899, just one month after his 15th birthday. Records show him to have been an above average scholar with good attendance, apart from the absence connected with the incident related previously. Ironically, in the light of his later pioneering work in the field of agriculture, he was marked down under the subject headed Agriculture in his school report.

As Harry learned to read, his lively mind sought to widen his knowledge and gain some entertainment through books. However the reading of books other than the Bible and approved Christian texts was strictly forbidden and he, along with some of his sisters, had to resort to under the blanket reading in defiance of this edict, sometimes suffering a beating as a result. In later years Harry had eyesight troubles and these clandestine readings may have initiated such problems. One author that he particularly enjoyed was Rudyard Kipling and later in life he would astonish listeners with his recitations of long passages from Kipling's poetry and prose.

Ever since he left school at fifteen Harry had worked on the farm, but he had never liked farm life and, although wiry and determined, he was of small stature and lightly built which did not fit well with the relentless and heavy work that farming then entailed. Harry had become friendly with his father's ploughman, a Jimmy Ferguson, and observing him one day wrestling with a heavy horse-drawn plough he remarked with clearly serious concern in his voice, "I think it's murderous work, I would never do it".

As Harry reached adolescence, that restless stage which has always existed but was perhaps not so well understood in those times, his resentment of the rigid lifestyle on the farm, his questioning of the dogmatic religious strictures given out during Bible readings at home and in lengthy meeting hall sermons grew day by day, increasingly leading to noisy clashes with his father and visiting preachers. It was a tense time for him.

Jimmy the ploughman was a keen fisherman in his limited free time and Harry, always curious, went with him to nearby Lough Aghery to see what it was all about. He quickly appreciated the tranquillity and the skill of the sport and found great relaxation on the rod, especially after a tiring day on the farm. Jimmy was also a member of a small group of musicians who played at local dances. Harry got wind of these activities and from time to time, despite the Brethren's very strong edict against dancing, found a way to take part in these sinful frivolities. In later years he recalled and still enjoyed hearing the old Irish tunes and rhythms, and the Music Hall ditties of those early stolen entertainments.

During these formative years significant developments in public transport were becoming more apparent about the countryside. After the invention of the pneumatic tyre in 1889, the safety bicycle, which had at first appeared in 1875 equipped with solid tyres, now took off in a big way, becoming readily available to large numbers of the population as a useful and enjoyable method of transport, while in 1895, following the invention of the 4-stroke internal combustion engine, a few cars and motorcycles were beginning to appear on the roads of Ulster, although initially only affordable by well off individuals. These mechanical devices were the ground breaking (all too literally!) technology of that age and as such were of particular interest to the youth of the day, offering the challenge and excitement of something new, and the opportunity to satisfy the youthful lust for speed.

Joe, Harry's older brother by 4 years, although not as radical as Harry in his makeup, had not reconciled himself to life on the Growell farm and was seeking a career with some engineering content. It is also probable that as his father was still relatively young and active on the farm, Joe realised that he would just be another farm worker for many years into the future. The ability of the farm to sustain their large family must also have been a factor in his decision.

Joe was fascinated by the new modes of transport just beginning to appear on the roads but as yet there were no real opportunities for employment in the trades associated with them. However the opportunities for anyone with a mechanical inclination were considerable at that time as there were a number of highly mechanised textile mills relatively close by and, as will be seen, industry was booming in Belfast just 15 miles away.

Joe Ferguson,
the progressive
businessman, in 1909

The effects of the Industrial Revolution had by now matured in Ulster, resulting in a tremendous concentration and growth of industry and commerce in the city of Belfast. While the first linen mills had been situated along the rivers Bann and Lagan in County Down, by around 1900 there were very many large mills in Belfast itself, carrying out all the various spinning and finishing processes associated with linen, and Belfast had become the largest linen centre in the world. Servicing these mills and other industries at home and worldwide were the large and innovative engineering works of James Mackie & Company and Combe-Barbour Ltd. The output of the shipbuilding industry, essentially now represented by the shipyards of Harland & Wolff and Workman Clark & Company, was such that Belfast was now also the world's largest manufacturer of ships. Harland & Wolff had just completed the liner Oceanic II for the White Star Line, which at that time was the largest and most luxurious liner in the world. Its success would lead on to a long line of fine ships for that company, including the Titanic and the Olympic. The Belfast Ropeworks, started up to service the needs of Harland

& Wolff, had expanded by 1900 to be the world's biggest rope-works, while Davison's 'Sirocco Works' led the world in the design and manufacture of industrial fans, which were used for tea drying in Asia and for large scale ventilation systems worldwide.

John Dunlop had by now established a factory in Belfast to manufacture pneumatic tyres, while Gallahers, already recognized for the excellence of their tobacco products, would in 1902 commence production of cigarettes, making them an internationally famous brand name.

By 1900 the Irish Distillery at Connswater, the Avoniel nearby and Dunvilles at Grosvenor were exporting 60 percent of Ireland's whiskey production, mainly through Belfast Port which was by now the premier port in Ireland.

This gives some idea of the potential opportunities for employment available to Joe and, accepting that his first preference for a career in the Motor Trade was not yet practical, he took up an apprenticeship in 1895 in one of Belfast's two premier engineering works, Combe-Barbour's of North Howard Street, Belfast.

During his apprenticeship period Joe kept a watchful eye on the progress of the motoring industry which was gathering momentum with more vehicles, both steam and petrol powered, were appearing on the roads. The first motor agency and garage in Ulster, and probably in the whole of Ireland, was started up in Chichester Street, Belfast in 1899 under the title 'The Northern Motor Company', and around the same time Joe received his first driving lesson on a Locomobile steam car. As he reached the end of his apprenticeship in 1901 it seemed clear that there were now promising opportunities in this new industry.

It must be remembered that at that time motorcars were very expensive machines and were owned mainly by wealthy land-owners, industrialists, and a few professional men. These individuals were unlikely to be inclined to lift the bonnet and get their hands dirty and, even if they had done, the mysteries of the internal combustion engine would have been beyond them, as indeed it would have been for most of the population. Many of these owners already employed grooms to look after their horses and ponies and to drive them about. These same grooms were now being required to take on the new motorcar, an entirely different beast. Engines were still relatively primitive and temperamental, while the early tyres struggled to protect the inner tubes from the rigours of the poor road surfaces of the day. So it took some time before these grooms were capable of handling the new technology. Clearly this situation alone was the basis for motor businesses, while the acquisition of an Agency for one of the few motorcars then on the market tied their customers into a steady flow of maintenance and repair.

On completion of his apprenticeship in autumn 1901, Joe, with a small amount of financial help from his father, was able to join with two other ex-apprentices from Combe-Barbour, Stewart Hamilton and James McKee, to form the 'Hamilton Partnership' offering tool making, development engineering and vehicle servicing from premises at 43 Shankill Road, Belfast.* While at Combe-Barbour, Joe had worked closely with Hamilton and McKee on improvements to steam-powered engines which they were now able to develop and take on to patenting.

*Although these premises, situated in the block between Hudson Street and McTier Street just above Peter's Hill survived the Blitz of 1941, they disappeared in the later re-development of the Shankill area in the 1960s.

Very quickly, as a result of their expert and thorough work, they acquired a reputation for reliability and their business thrived. This should not come as a surprise, for all three were clearly talented engineers and Joe, although later overshadowed by his younger brother's great successes had in addition the drive and good business sense that enabled this initial enterprise to prosper.

Back at Growell, Harry was still toiling away on the farm and growing increasingly disenchanted with his existence. At this time many young people were emigrating to the New World, with the attraction of plentiful employment and the apparent opportunity for those with drive and ability to do well, and all within countries that valued the freedoms of thought and of expression. Although quite an outgoing personality, his thrusting and sometimes acerbic attitude at times hindered the making of friends; indeed even at home he never managed very close relationships with his brothers and sisters. He had confidence in himself and his abilities, but perhaps suspected that if he remained within the traditionally-minded local environment, his rather mercurial nature and his limited social graces might be handicaps to progress, whereas in a developing New World they could be a positive advantage. Harry came to the decision to emigrate and started making plans to go to Canada. It was a big decision.

On an autumn Sunday in 1902, Joe arrived at Lake House, alerted discreetly by their mother of Harry's intentions. He found Harry in a sombre mood. He put it to Harry that he needed a driver to help him in the growing business and offered him an apprenticeship with the firm. Harry didn't hesitate. Of recent times he had grown more and more interested in cars and motorcycles but no opportunity to get involved with them had yet shown itself. Here was his chance and he grasped it. He packed a bag and later that very same evening he walked the six miles to Hillsborough railway station with Joe and took the train to Belfast. A new horizon was opening up.

NB It is interesting to note that Joe, despite running a business at least in part associated with vehicles, clearly did not yet own one himself.

Motorbike Man

The premises of J. B.
Ferguson Automobile
Engineers at 41 Little
Donegall Street and
17 Union Street, circa
1904. The Union
Street building stood
virtually unchanged
until demolished for
redevelopment in
2008. Compare with
much larger premises
in Chicester Street
to which the firm
moved in 1907.

Inset: the front of the
premises on Little
Donegall Street

Full of enthusiasm, Harry set to work to learn all he could about vehicles and their engines. Used to the hard and varied work on the farm he was prepared to turn his hand to anything that needed to be done, but very quickly he found that he had a real knack for tuning engines, surprising and rather embarrassing his more experienced brother by quickly correcting the irregular working of the workshop's static gas engine, which had been giving trouble for months on end.

Early in 1903 the Hamilton Partnership broke up. Joe was more interested in the vehicle side of the work while Hamilton and McKee had a greater interest in general engineering. Hamilton and McKee remained at 43 Shankill Road, while Joe moved to larger premises at 41 Little Donegall Street, Belfast* under the title 'J. B. Ferguson Automobile Engineers'. Unfortunately for Hamilton and McKee, the demand for general engineering was insufficient to sustain their enterprise. Hamilton soon came back to work with Joe again at J. B. Ferguson, while McKee joined William Barbour & Sons Ltd. at Hilden near Lisburn, although four years later in 1907 he too rejoined Joe at J. B. Ferguson Limited, as it had then become.

*These premises initially only frontaged Little Donegall Street, but soon expanded to include 17 Union Street, new premises on the corner of the recently constructed Union Street. Number 41 Little Donegall Street has subsequently been re-built. The Union Street property survived largely unchanged until early 2008, but has since been demolished and by early 2009 re-development had commenced.

Joe was a strict disciplinarian and paid a lot of attention to the accuracy and quality of the work turned out by the workshop, further improving the good reputation previously established in the first workshop. He was a serious-minded man and was ambitious for the development of his business. Realising that the key to success was good management, he gave close supervision to his staff and ensured that they were well equipped. He had a comprehensive electrical power system installed in the workshop, with electric lighting throughout, and it was the first motor workshop in Belfast to use electric power drills and to have the inspection pit electrically lit.

Over the next few years Harry became totally involved in all aspects of the motor business, from the practical basics of the correct use of tools to the complete repair and overhaul of a vehicle. He worked side by side with the mechanics and fitters and learned to understand their skills, while they in turn came to appreciate his natural ability and his thorough and dedicated attitude to everything he was working on. In the autumn of 1906 there was a much heralded opening of the just completed Belfast College of Technology and Harry saw the opportunity to supplement his practical training with the theoretical knowledge that might be gained there. He enrolled in the first College intake on 11th September 1906, with Machine Drawing as his principal subject. In the light of his many future engineering achievements it is remarkable that this was the only technical training he ever received.

FIRST ISSUE

MUNICIPAL TECHNICAL INSTITUTE, Belfast.

SESSION 1906-1907. (Sixth Session.)

Ticket No. 2

Rotation No. 528

ENTRANCE FORM. (FOR ALL CLASSES) EXCEPT ART CLASSES.

NOTES AND HINTS FOR STUDENTS.

(1.) You are earnestly advised to read the Notes relative to Courses of Study, which are given on the back of this Form.

(2.) Before applying in the Office for a Class Ticket, consult the Teacher and make quite sure that you are sufficiently prepared to take up with advantage to yourself the Course of Study you wish to enter upon. This is important, as **Tickets are not transferable from one class to another**. In the Time Table you will find a note stating the hours at which Teachers may be consulted.

(3.) Fill up the Entrance Forms for the subjects comprising your course of study, answering in full the queries printed in red. The particulars asked for are those specified by the Department of Agriculture and Technical Instruction, and are required for official use only.

(4.) Ask the Teachers to initial the Entrance Forms.

(5.) A separate Form must be filled up for each class comprised in a *Special* course, but only one form for a Preparatory course or an Introductory course.

(6.) It is a condition for admission at the Fee named in the Time Table that the Student shall attend regularly, and conform to the rules as to Home Work, and as to attendance at Examination when one is held.

(7.) A Student who does not wish to comply with the regulations as to Courses of Study will be exempted on payment of treble the class fee.

(7.) You will greatly assist the Office Staff—especially in the very busy opening days of the Session—if you will have the **exact** amount of your Fees ready when applying for class tickets. Much time is necessarily occupied when change has to be given.

Surname -	Ferguson
Christian Name or Names (in full).	Harry George
Private Address -	46 Lonsdale St
Age (last birthday) -	21

Date of Birth 4th November 1884
(day of month) (month) (year)

Occupation -	Automobile Engineer
Employer's Name (A Student under age not engaged in business should give Father's Name)	J.B. Ferguson & Co
Employer's Address -	41 43 Little Donegal St
Standard or Grade in which enrolled at date of leaving School, or standard of education since reached -	6th Past Student.

(Subject.)   (Grade.)

| State the subjects you have chosen for your Course of Study - | Machine Drawing. Applied Mechanics. Practical Mathematics |
| Date of Application for Ticket - | 11th September 190 6 |

THESE COLUMNS ARE FOR OFFICE USE ONLY.

No. Lns.	H. W.	Ex. R.			Pr.	Remarks.	Subject for which Ticket is required.	Singe or Grade.	Which Class (when more than one).	FEE.	IF YOU HAVE STUDIED THIS SUBJECT BEFORE, STATE		
G	A	P	A	Ex. B.	St.	Cl.					INSTITUTE ATTENDED.	Year.	Stage of Subject Studied.	Your Success at Exam.
							Machine Drawing	1	4	2/6				

Entry Approved by ____ (Teacher.)   Verified by ____   Ticket issued by ____   Cash received by ____

Quota. Printer Belfast (t.g.06.)

Harry's entrance form for the first intake of the Municipal Technical Institute, Belfast, later Belfast College of Technology, on 11th September, 1906. Note the tuition fee of 2 shillings and 6 pence, today's 25p.

Another student on the course was John Lloyd Williams. Harry had already met John Williams when, as will be related later, they both took part in motor cycle events. Born in 1885 in Yorkshire, John was just a year younger than Harry and had been taken on as an engineering apprentice by Harland & Wolff in 1902, the same year Harry had started with Joe. They became firm friends and within a few years, business colleagues. Harry had a strong and confident personality that could bring respect and tacit approval, but he lacked the vital spark of humour that can humanise, ease and establish relationships. John Williams supplied this missing ingredient, which, along with his genuine regard for Harry and his appreciation of his burgeoning talents, cemented their long friendship. When Harry came under pressure, either self-imposed or otherwise, John could ease the tension with light banter or leg pulling and other diversionary tactics.

In addition to his instinctive mechanical talent, Harry provided a complementary element to the running of the motor business with his more thrusting and lively make up. He was never happier than when he was behind the wheel, although his spirited driving when returning cars to their owners had, on occasion, caused expensive outcomes. However as the customers got to know him they appreciated his technical expertise and the care and attention he paid to the maintenance of their vehicles.

This youthful pleasure in driving, married to his thrusting nature, meant that very soon Harry was looking for opportunities to express himself in speed and in competition. Fortunately things were moving to satisfy this strong desire.

At this time the bicycle, still in its heyday, had stimulated a whole recreational and sporting demand, which resulted in the formation of many cycle clubs under the overall umbrella of the Irish Cyclists' Association (ICA) which organised cycle runs, time trials and cycle races, while specialist magazines like *The Irish Wheelman* and *The Irish Cyclist* came on the market. Similarly, as the number of motor cars increased, specialist motoring magazines such as *Motor, Autocar* and *The Irish Motor News* were published and associations like the Automobile Club of Britain and Ireland (ACB&I) and the Irish Automobile Club (IAC) were formed to look after the interests of motorists and to organise motoring events.

Meanwhile the availability of motor cycles was growing rapidly. Motorcycles were less expensive than cars to buy and to run, and appealed greatly to a younger and perhaps more sporty clientele than that of the motor car. It was not long therefore before a demand for motorcycle clubs and associations became apparent. In March 1902 the Motor Cycle Union of Ireland (MCUI) was formed in Dublin, and in January 1903 an affiliated branch, the Ulster Centre, was inaugurated in Belfast. The first President of the MCUI was John Boyd Dunlop of pneumatic tyre fame, while a prime mover in both these developments was the Belfast born editor of *The Irish Wheelman,* James C. Percy, whose name will appear again later in the story of Harry Ferguson's flying endeavours.

In the early days there was often an overlap at events organised by the ICA and the Ulster Centre, with races for both bicycles and motorcycles at each of their events. Indeed a number of the more thrusting racing cyclists graduated to motor cycles. For example in August 1902, when the first motorcycle race in Ulster was held at the Ballymena Bicycle Club's cement cycling track, now the site of Ballymena Showgrounds, one of the four starters was a Joseph Cordner of Lurgan, who had previously been a very successful bicycle racer. As will be seen later on in this account, this Joe Cordner features further in the section dealing with Harry Ferguson's flying contemporaries. In addition to the mixing of bicycles and motor cycles at some early events, and prior to the formation of the Ulster Automobile Club, the Ulster Centre in their later fixtures offered classes for both motor cycles and motor cars.

Nowadays most of us set out in our cars without a thought that it might let us down; there are five year guarantees, it will start instantly on turning the key and hold the road comfortably and safely (depending on our driving!), while punctures are almost a thing of the past. That past was just 100 years ago when Harry was starting to drive cars and ride motor cycles. At that time cars had temperamental engines and with only rudimentary springing they were heavy to steer and to drive. They had to be crank started with the starting handle, which in itself was often a struggle and not for the faint-hearted. The early motorcycles were initially little more than bicycles with engines added. With light tyres, inadequate brakes, little or no springing, belt transmissions and hand gear changing they were quite a handful. The main roads were at best uneven trackways formed on the macadam system using layers of progressively smaller broken stones topped with stone chippings and gravel, prepared and finished largely by hand, or if available, by horse-drawn rollers, a construction barely suitable even for the horse-drawn traffic it was originally designed to serve. The wearing surface was susceptible to washout under heavy rain and from wheel damage, requiring a constant maintenance that was not always available. Although sealing the wearing surface of roads with tar was introduced into Ulster around 1903, at first only urban roads were thus treated, and the main roads outside of towns remained as described. Minor roads were little more than country lanes. It is not surprising therefore that problems arose on the roads, indeed setting out on a car or motorcycle journey was a bit of an adventure or at the very least, a challenge. Punctures in particular were a serious problem.

The first full macadam surface in the whole of Ireland, a one mile stretch of the Belfast to Lisburn road at Dunmurry, was completed by the engineering firm George Gregg and Son of Larne in 1909, and they were very quickly at the forefront of extending the use of what became commonly known as tarmac all over the island, although it was not until 1914 or so that steamrollers began to be commonly used, with County Councils only starting to operate them widely in the early twenties.

It can therefore be appreciated that the sporting events arranged at that time by the MCU were quite rigorous, although they would hardly seem so today. A 200 mile Reliability Trial from Belfast to Derry via the Antrim Coast Road and back by Maghera would be wee buns nowadays, but at that time it was fraught with punctures, overheating, and electrical problems etc and, with no garages along the roads, it was self-help, with engine adjustments and puncture repairs carried out at the roadside. In an early Reliability Trial one motorcycle competitor, J. S. Garret, had to repair twelve punctures in the eight miles between Dunmurry and Hillsborough before he gave up!

Harry's attraction to speed, combined with his engine tuning talent, led him to start taking part in these competitive events for motorcycles and later in motor cars. Both brothers were just into their twenties and, although Harry was by all accounts the more sport conscious, Joe also took part in some of the early events. It is thought that Harry convinced him that such participation would be good for business, rather than it being Joe's natural inclination. As will be seen Harry soon achieved considerable success in these events, with his name appearing in local newspapers such as *Ireland's Saturday Night,* Ulster's most popular sporting paper, and in the cycling and motoring magazines now being published. Not only were Harry's successes newsworthy, but the enthusiastic, competitive style of his riding and driving and his forthright comments after events combined to make him a focus of attention, all good publicity for the J. B. Ferguson business.

Harry all kitted up to take part in a reliability trial on his Minerva circa 1907. Note the relatively light wheels and tyres, the belt drive and the retention of foot pedals.

The Ulster Centre's first 200 mile Reliability Trial from Belfast to Derry and back, as previously referred to, took place on 19th July 1904. It was solely for motorcycles and Joe took part on a 2½hp Excelsior. He came a creditable second behind the very experienced John Burney on a more powerful 3½hp Royal Enfield. Joe reported no serious problems other than losing himself a few times in some of the towns he passed through. There is no mention of Harry taking part in this event. This was probably because it was little over a year since he was apprenticed to the firm and he would still have been considered a junior there. It was a time when the business was still getting established and it might not have been felt sensible to field two entrants, with the added expense that would entail.

In February 1905 the Ulster Centre held their AGM, with Joe being elected on to the committee. On 8th April they started off their 1905 season with a hill climb at Gilnahirk. About a dozen started, and Harry not only won the event on a 2¾hp Minerva but did the fastest time, despite competing against more powerful machines. A Leslie Wilkinson came third on a Riley motorcycle. Leslie Wilkinson had a bicycle shop in Main Street Hillsborough and later became a key assistant to Harry during his flying days and afterwards.

Ireland's Saturday Night commented, 'the hill is about one of the toughest that could be chosen, in fact it erred in this direction, because some of the motors, while suitable enough for average work, could not negotiate it without the aid of pedalling'.

On 29th April 1905, ten competitors took part in the Ulster Centre's hill climb at Central Avenue Bangor, with Joe on a

Minerva finishing one second behind the winner. Both brothers competed in the next hill climb on 18th May, also in Bangor, with Joe winning and Harry finishing fifth.

Saturday 3rd June 1905 saw the Ulster Centre's 100 mile Reliability Trial, Belfast to Dundalk and back. Harry and Leslie Wilkinson were among the starters in this nonstop run. Although they both finished well up the order they were penalised, as they

'got off and ran beside their machines uphill, which ranks as a stop although the engine never ceased'!

The next Reliability Trial organised by the Ulster Centre was for their newly acquired, magnificent solid silver Muratti Trophy. This took place on 13th and 14th July 1905 and covered a total of 400 miles, Belfast to Dublin and back on the first day and Belfast to Derry and back on the second. Joe entered on a Minerva and Harry rode a James-Minerva.

NB. The Minerva company in Belgium were one of the foremost motorcycle manufacturers of the day. They supplied complete motorcycles fitted with their own engines or sold their engines

Harry (right) with his pushbike on Queen's Parade in Bangor, where he was attending a hill-climb event over nearby Central Avenue on 29th April 1905. Joe came second on a Minerva motorcycle similar to the one in the photograph

The beautifully detailed and very valuable solid silver Muratti Trophy awarded to the winners of of the 200 mile Reliability Trials for motorbikes

separately to other manufacturers such as James, for incorporation in frames of that factory's own particular design. In 1905 J. B. Ferguson had an agency for Minerva motor cycles and were advertising their 2¾ hp version for sale at £29 (c. £2,500 today). Leslie Wilkinson, and later John Williams, rode Minervas in these early motorcycle events. It would seem likely that they bought their machines from J. B. Ferguson & Co., which could have been their introduction to Harry and the beginning of their long associations with him.

The report of the event describes Joe as progressing well (with only 4 or 5 punctures!) until disaster struck on the second day when, just out of Derry on the return to Belfast, he was knocked off his motorcycle by an excitable and careless cyclist spectator. Joe suffered quite bad facial injuries and his machine was too badly damaged to continue. Leslie Wilkinson, however, completed the course and came in third. Harry was a non-finisher.

On 29th July 1905, due to appalling weather, the Ulster Centre's trial for the St. Mars Cup over the usual 200 mile Belfast-Derry-Belfast course had to be abandoned. But due to the perseverance of Harry Ferguson and James Stewart, who managed to get as far as Limavady, they were both rewarded with handsome prizes. At the time of cancellation Harry was in first place.

Harry took part in the Ulster Centre's hill climb at Gilnahirk on 28th August 1905 on a Minerva. He recorded the second fastest time, three seconds behind the well-known R. Ireton on a more powerful Riley motorcycle.

At the Ulster Centre's AGM in February 1906, Harry was elected on to the committee. The Ulster Centre's first hill climb of the year was held over the ¾ mile course at Gilnahirk on 7th April.

Harry came first with a time of 1 minute 4.5 seconds, riding a Riley motorcycle.

The second 1906 hill climb took place at Central Avenue, Bangor on 21st April, and on this occasion Joe was the winner in 46.4 secs.

In the second 400 mile, two day, Reliability Trial for the Muratti Trophy on 13th and 14th July 1906, Harry came a close second behind a very experienced English rider F. Hulbert, despite at the last minute having to start on a brand new Minerva fitted with non-competition tyres. This was kindly loaned to Harry by a customer when the machine Harry had on order was not delivered in time. The cycling correspondent of *Ireland's Saturday Night* considered his performance as probably the best of the event, commenting,

'the machine was ordinary stock pattern, which had not covered fifty miles before it started in the event. It was only fitted with plain tyres, and how he managed to keep an absolutely 'green'

Harry, left, with his Minerva at the Crown and Shamrock hostelry on the Antrim Road at Mallusk at the end of a reliability trial engine going without heating troubles and preserved his equilibrium on the greasy roads the other competitors don't know'.

Just behind Harry, scoring 155 points to Harry's 160, was James Stewart, who was becoming Harry's closest local rival and, as will be seen, the subject of a sporting controversy.

Another Competitor in this event was A.V. Blake of Magheramorne near Larne, who rode a 2¾ hp Coventry Eagle. A.V. Blake will appear later in this account as another of Harry's flying contemporaries.

On 25th August 1906 Harry took part in a nonstop Reliability Trial from Belfast (Balmoral) to Castlewellan with a hill climb at Ballybannon Hill, again on a Minerva. The event, which also included motor cars, set the time for completion of the 43 mile course at 2 hrs 9 mins, an average of 20 mph! Harry came overall fourth on his 2¾ hp Minerva behind a 3½ hp Rover motorcycle and two motor cars of 16 and 11 hp respectively. In the hill climb section he was first in the motorcycle class, 0.8 seconds in front of James Stewart on a Triumph. John Williams also competed in the event on another 2¾ hp Minerva. This is the first time that Harry and John Williams are recorded as taking part in the same event.

The Ulster Centre organised a hill climb at Gilnahirk on 22nd September 1906. On this occasion there were separate classes for motor cars and motorcycles, each with handicaps based on the stroke and bore of engine and overall weight, with penalties for previous wins. Joe entered with a 5 hp Peugeot motor car while Harry entered on a 2¾ hp Minerva motor cycle. Joe was unplaced but Harry was awarded first place, made fastest time overall and was fastest even when his handicap penalty was taken into account. So it was not surprising that when the *Ireland's Saturday Night's* cycling correspondent reporting the event commented that, *'the first three finishers were clearly far too liberally treated by the handicapper'*, Harry's competitive nature and sense of fairness immediately surfaced and he wrote to the newspaper protesting. Basically he said that the handicapper had done his best to be fair and accurate and that no matter what handicap he

would have been given, he would have competed vigorously. He went on to say,

'there is no person I assure you, who does more for the Union than myself, and I can easily grasp the fact that it would not be for its benefit that one man should win all the time. I do not desire this, but what I desire is that when I make a fair performance (and you will yourself admit that Saturday's was by no means a bad one on a standard 2¾ hp machine) that it is not made light of. Of course, I am well aware of the fact that every competitor has not the same facilities for putting his machine in order for such a contest as this as I myself have, and with this in view, I do not object in the least being penalised. At the same time, I think you will yourself agree with me that the man who gives his machine the most attention and does not leave the merest detail undone that give him a few seconds, is the man who should win, other things being equal'.

The full contents of Harry's letter are given in Appendix 2.

The newspaper printed Harry's letter in full and their reporter then went on to justify his original comment with great strength and with what seems to be a certain degree of personal animosity

The Gilnahirk hill climb on 22nd September 1906 started from the front of Gilnahirk Presbyterian Church. Harry, seen on the right with his 2¾ hp Minerva, was placed first ahead of R. Ireton and A.F. Craig. It was following this event that the handicapping controversy arose towards Harry (Appendix 3). One has the feeling that the reporter's response, which is a bit over the top, may in part have been the result of a clash of personalities between a lively reporter and a bullish Harry with his assertive reputation, rather than due to the contents of Harry's letter, which are not overly combative.

After his initial remarks directed at Harry, the reporter gets to the crux of the comments in his original report, which in fact were not unreasonable. He was making the point that it was unfair for truly amateur private owners to have to compete with professional riders on 'works' machines as long as the handicapping stuck rigidly to the nominal stroke, bore and weight of the machine and took no account of sophisticated fine tuning and other adjustments that could be made by the professional entrants. While Harry clearly did have the assistance of J. B. Ferguson's facilities and mechanics, it is certain that most of the expertise and much of the work on his machine would have been his own and he would have felt, not unfairly, that it was not a 'works' machine as such. Indeed it is fair to say that at that time the knowledge of engines and their tuning was still in its infancy and the difference between professional and amateur preparation would not have been as great as it is today.

The Ulster Centre clearly took note of the above exchange of views and offered a degree of separation for entrants by creating classes for 'Private Owners' and 'Open to all Members' in their first hill climb event in 1907 on 6th April at Bangor. Harry entered two Minervas, his last season's 2¾ hp machine and a new 3½ hp model. He recorded fastest time overall and was fastest under handicap on the 2¾ hp machine, but surprisingly could only manage ninth on the more powerful Minerva.

The Dublin Centre of the MCUI held speed trials on Portmarnock Strand, Co. Dublin on 27th April. Harry came first in the One Mile Member's Handicap race on a Minerva, and finished second in the final of the Ten Miles Handicap event, behind C. W. Smith on a Triumph.

The Ulster Centre held a 63 mile Reliability Trial to Ballycastle on 11th May and, although Harry entered to ride his Minerva, he was a non-starter. In their Castlewellan hill climb on 18th May he came fourth in the Open Class riding the Minerva.

The Reliability Trial for the Muratti Trophy in 1907 took place on 5th and 6th August in atrocious weather. Harry and James Stewart, regularly close rivals, came equal first after the gruelling 400 mile, two-day event. It was proposed that they should re-run the Derry to Belfast section of the course to decide the winner or that they each hold the Trophy for six months. Harry, with a typically uncompromising stance refused both options, forcefully claiming himself to be the winner on the basis that Stewart had worked on his machine at the Belfast and Limavady controls. He lodged an official protest and Stewart made a counter protest. Both protests were dismissed and they were again offered a re-run. When Harry again refused, the Ulster Centre awarded the Trophy to Stewart. This disagreement was covered widely in the Press and Appendix 4, quoting from the *ISN's* full report on the subject, gives a flavour of the strength of feelings aroused in the local motor sports arena. Harry truly seems to be pushing his luck a bit too far on this occasion and cannot be said to come out of the argument on the right side. Although this controversy again highlights Harry's extremely competitive nature, there is always the suspicion that Harry encouraged, or at least enjoyed, such controversy, perhaps knowing quite well that all publicity is good publicity.

The Ulster Centre's last event of 1908 was a hill climb at Central Avenue, Bangor on 3rd October. In the class for motor cars Harry came first in his 14/16 Argyll. In the Open Class for motorcycles he was scratch rider on a 5½ hp Rex and finished fourth, although he made fastest time in 35.5 seconds. In the light of later comments on Harry's early involvement in flight, it is interesting to see that as late as October 1908 he was still participating fully in motoring events.

It must not be forgotten that as well as taking part in all these motoring events Harry still had his day job, and it is certain that Joe initially exercised plenty of control over these activities. Although they had their differences, Joe could see Harry's talent and his potential. Joe fully recognised the publicity benefits accruing from Harry's sporting successes, but was level-headed enough to know that the benefits gained would only be retained if the quality of their products and workmanship were also maintained. As Harry quickly gained practical experience on the shop floor he steadily moved towards an overseeing position, eventually being formally appointed Works Manager. While continuing the tight supervision of staff instituted by his brother he devised working systems, such as tool management and specialisation, to ensure efficient working. Harry even insisted that all the mechanics carry a small notebook in the left hand pocket of their overalls to record any information or ideas gained from their working experience. The workshop was one area where the two brothers shared similar attitudes. They both paid great attention to the technical quality of the work being done and they put great emphasis on presentation. The workshops and all the staff had to be neat and tidy at all times and vehicles had to be returned to their owners gleaming like new. Harry himself always dressed neatly in a business suit with a white shirt and a starched collar and a tie, and very often with a flower in his buttonhole. As has been said, in those days the motoring events in which he took part were no picnic, with the unpaved roads and the resulting on-course tyre changes etc., but even here he seems to manage to retain his neat appearance, as can be seen in contemporary photographs.

From 1903 when J. B. Ferguson & Co. had moved to Little Donegall Street there had been a steady growth in their business. Much of this growth was a reflection of the ever increasing demand for cars and motorcycles, but the high reputation for quality and service that the firm had achieved under Joe's thorough management also played a major part, while Harry's projection of the Ferguson name through his successes in motorsports and perhaps even through their controversial reporting, must also have made a significant contribution. Although Joe had been first to take part in the early motorcycle events, and with some success, after the September 1906 Gilnahirk hill climb in which he drove a Peugeot car, he decided to concentrate on the development of his business interests, and left the competitive activities to Harry.

Harry at the wheel of
an early car outside
the J. B. Ferguson
premises at 41 Little
Donegall Street.
Belfast, circa 1905

Due to the continual growth of the J. B. Ferguson business and its reputation they were able to acquire the agency for Argyll cars, one of the foremost British makes of that time and very popular with Irish motorists. As part of the arrangements associated with this agency, Harry spent several weeks at the Argyll works studying all aspects of their vehicles. The acquisition of this agency was related to plans Joe had been formulating for some time, to move to larger and more prestigious premises. Joe Ferguson was recognised as an able and ambitious businessman, and it clear that he was planning a major step forward.

Fortuitously in 1905 a long standing entertainment facility at 60-62 Chichester Street, known as the Imperial Hippodrome and Circus had closed down and these premises, along with some adjoining property, came on the market. This location was exactly what Joe had in mind and he started negotiations to purchase all the properties between No. 60 and No. 76 on Chichester Street, a frontage occupied in recent times by the new Victoria Centre. From what is known of the original Hippodrome, the developed J. B. Ferguson building indicates a virtual re-build of the entire premises. This was an enormous commitment and clearly proves Joe's strong ambition and his business acumen.

Prior to J. B. Ferguson Ltd. gaining the agency for Argyll cars, Harry spent some time in the Argyll Works studying their products in detail. The Argyll was a top class car of its day, much liked by Irish motorists

The result of this investment was motor trading facilities second to none, and in line with this expansion, Joe started to reorganise the business as a Limited Company. During 1906 the building works proceeded and by March 1907, as they neared completion the change to a Limited Liability Company was ratified. The legal contract setting up the company, dated 26th March, gives it as having a nominal Capital of £6,000, divided into 6,000 shares of £1. Joe was the principal shareholder and Managing Director, and Argyll Motors were major investors, with Alec Govan of Argyll being a director along with Harry, two local merchants F.S. Wilson and J.C. Nixon and two employees W.S. Fennel and J.H. Canning. A similarly dated document also appoints Harry formally as *the first Works Manager* at an annual salary of £125, paid quarterly, with a 10% bonus of the nett profits after payment of Dividends and Tax. It further stated that as Works Manager he *shall carry out the assignments set out from time to time and obey orders from time to time of the Board of Directors of the Company or their authorised Manager*. (Although this was probably standard legal language, one could be tempted to think it was anticipating the possibility of some obstreperous behaviour by Harry!)

In June 1907 J.B. Ferguson Limited moved into their much larger new premises in Chichester Street, indeed they were far and away the most prestigious motor business premises in Belfast and probably in the whole of Ireland. At No. 60 there was the vehicle access to and from the workshop at the rear. The remainder of the frontage was occupied by a large showroom and the main customer entrance hallway, giving access to extensive offices on the upper floors. The workshop behind ran the full length of the Chichester Street frontage and had a partial-mezzanine working level along the rear wall. The additional facilities now available not only allowed for the expected increase in their basic sales, servicing and repair trade, but enabled the business to provide a motor hire service and a very popular driving school.

NB. These premises were extensively modernised in the 1930s, with leased-out shops provided at ground floor level and additional floors of offices for letting fitted out above. In this form J. B. Ferguson Limited occupied the premises into the 1960s.

During the hectic transfer period in 1907 and into 1908 Harry, as Works Manager, must have been kept very busy and when his motorsport activities are taken into account it would seem that his commitment to motoring in all its aspects was his whole life. But fresh horizons seem to be appearing before him.

For the various Ferguson locations in Belfast, see map in Appendix 5.

The progressive expansion of the J. B. Ferguson motor business, once established in Chichester Street, is seen in the advert. Here lessons in driving and in motor car maintenance are on offer, in addition to their sales, service and car hire trade

Flight:
The New Challenge

According to an interview in *The Irish Motor News* of 16th October 1909, Harry started considering the possibilities of building an aeroplane towards the end of 1908. This is rather surprising, as has been shown, his life at that time appears to have been entirely wrapped up in all aspects of the motor vehicle and even as late as October 1908 he is competing in a hill climb at Bangor with his usual vigour and success. However it was his nature to be searching out challenges, particularly those that combined mechanical expertise with a degree of excitement and it must have seemed to him that flying offered just such a challenge. It is therefore of interest here to consider the situation in aviation at that time and to see how news of its progress might have kindled his interest.

Despite the success of the Wright Brother in conquering the air on 17th December 1903 there was relatively little press coverage of the event worldwide or even in the USA itself. There were stirrings of activity in France but information largely remained within the flying fraternity. The Wrights worked away quietly perfecting their aircraft while attempting to negotiate comprehensive sales contracts with sceptical Governments. An astonishing four years elapsed with little emerging to stimulate the wider public's interest in aviation. During 1907 things began to move in France with the arrival of the Wrights in May, followed in August by their expert mechanic, Charles Taylor, bringing a series of crates containing the components of an aircraft and its engine.

A number of French enthusiasts, including Farman, Voisin, Bleriot etc, were now experimenting with aircraft designs and towards the end of 1907 early versions of their aircraft were appearing, although none truly displayed the studied understanding of aerodynamics already achieved by the Wrights. The Wrights' contract negotiations in Europe having failed, they returned to the USA in early November leaving the crates containing their aircraft at Le Havre unopened. So during 1907, few other than the aeronautical cognoscenti were aware of any progress that was being made.

In 1908 things started to speed up. Wilbur Wright arrived back in France in May and started to assemble the 1907 aircraft and its engine. A number of problems occurred and it was not until 8th August 1908 that he made his first flight at Hunadieres. His display, showing his complete control of the aircraft in the air, was a tremendous sensation and news of his flights quickly spread all over Europe and the UK, the event being covered in all the main newspapers of the day.

Towards the end of the 1908 Farman and Voisin in their bi-planes were also making short flights and more significantly in the light of Harry's eventual approach to aircraft design, Bleriot and Antoinette monoplanes were beginning to appear in a recognizable form and were achieving a little success.

Closer to home the first officially recognized aeroplane flight in England occurred on 16th October 1908 at Farnborough. This was made by the charismatic and publicity conscious Samuel Franklin Cody in an aeroplane of his own design. S.F. Cody was an expatriate American who in earlier years had toured all over Britain and Europe with his extremely popular and well known Wild West Show and so stories of his new flying activities were big news.

The year 1909 was a significant one for aviation. At the beginning of it the vast majority of the general public considered that flying was for the birds and that participants in this passing craze were at best eccentrics and at worst, mad. When the year was over the wider perception had changed to the recognition that aviation had a significant future.

Wilbur Wright continued to give demonstration flights, including passenger trips, in France and Italy until April 1909. Three particular passengers and observers of flights piloted by Wilbur were Charles Rolls of Rolls Royce fame, J.T.C. Moore –

Brabazon, later Lord Brabazon of Tara and a wealthy wine merchant, Griffith Brewer. All were ardent balloonists, or aeronauts as they were then called, and had bought balloons from the Short Brothers who had become the prime balloon manufacturers in Britain by that time. Rolls, Moore-Brabazon and Brewer, fired by their contacts with the Wright Brothers in France, were keen to see aviation developed in England and very quickly convinced the Short Brothers that the future of aviation lay in fixed-wing aircraft rather than balloons, and that they should be involved in that future. They then set about getting a commitment from the Wrights to allow their aeroplanes to be built in England. As well as Rolls and Moore-Brabazon, there were already several other wealthy men in England who had become interested in learning to fly and to buy aeroplanes and a search was made for a suitable flying ground where such activities could be centred.

Involved in this search, in addition to Griffith Brewer, was Frank McClean (later knighted Sir Francis for services to aviation), the son of a Belfast-born engineer who became extremely successful and wealthy in mining, canals and railways. A site at Leysdown on the Isle of Sheppey in Kent was chosen and very quickly, early in 1909, it became alive with would-be aviators. In order to facilitate progress, Frank McClean used his inherited wealth

37

to purchase the ground, and commissioned the Short Brothers to design and build an aeroplane for him. With this and other demands coming to hand the Short Brothers decided to move their aeroplane business from Battersea to Leysdown and built a small factory there for that purpose, on land leased to them by Frank McClean for a nominal rent. This is considered to have been the first factory in the world built exclusively for aeroplane construction and is the basis of the claim by Short Brothers to be the first aircraft manufacturers in the world. With Short Brothers established at Laysdown the Wright Brothers were brought over to see their facilities and to savour the general air of enthusiasm for aviation that existed there. The result of these efforts was the award of a contract to Shorts to build 6 Wright 'Flyers' for English customers, the very beginning of that firm's long and productive existence.

But back to Harry Ferguson and the stirrings of his interest in aviation. Both Rolls and Moore-Brabazon were leading members of the motoring fraternity, from which most of the earliest aviators came, and their activities received much publicity in the motoring magazines. There were no dedicated aeronautical publications in the UK in 1908, but the motoring magazines covered all of the more striking aeronautical happenings, in some cases carrying photographs and basic illustrations of the aircraft involved. With Harry's motoring interests he would certainly have been following the much publicised motoring exploits of Rolls and Brabazon covered by these periodicals, and would have seen their developing interest in ballooning and into flying. One can see how his interest in another exciting activity would have been quickly aroused. In 1909 *Autocar* weekly, sensing the need for a specialist aeronautical periodical, started the publication of a sister weekly, *Flight*. Harry is likely to have taken this magazine early on, if not at the beginning, as by November he was in correspondence with it seeking information on technical matters.

1909 was to be an eventful year for aviation, and by this time even the popular press was beginning to sit up and take notice of these activities and the journalistic opportunities they offered. Lord Northcliffe the owner of the *Daily Mail,* who had long had an interest in aviation, dispatched his special correspondent

Harry Harper to France to report on flying progress there. On the 6th June Harper managed to get taken up in an Antoinette monoplane at Chalons by a daring and charismatic pilot, Hubert Latham. The next day a dramatic account of his exciting experience was published in the *Daily Mail*. While Lord Northcliffe always had an eye on his newspaper's circulation figures, he was also genuinely concerned at English officialdom's lack of attention to aeronautical affairs. As a stimulus to English interest in aviation he announced his offer of a £1,000 prize for the first aeroplane flight between England and France. The Aero Club of London were to organize the event and official regulations were issued on 17th June 1909.

It should be remembered that £1,000 was a significant amount of money at that time, perhaps £100,000 in today's values, while the English Channel had an almost mythical importance in the strategic insularity of the British Isles far beyond the 21 miles of its width. To conquer this particular stretch of water would be a dramatic event of international significance.

This prize in itself is likely to have appealed to Harry's competitive spirit and he may have started to think really seriously about building an aircraft at this time, but if not, the dramatic events that followed the offer most certainly would have clinched it. On 28th June, Hubert Latham, registered his Antoinette monoplane as an entry for the prize, and on 19th July took off from Sangatte heading for Dover. Unfortunately after a relatively short time his engine started to misfire and he was forced to glide down on to the water, from where he was rescued still sitting in the cockpit calmly smoking a cigarette. He immediately signalled his intention of making a second attempt and ordered the preparation of another Antoinette. However on the same day Louis Bleriot announced that he would attempt the crossing in his Bleriot monoplane and soon arrived at Les Baraques near Calais. On 25th June he took off and, after a flight of 36 minutes 30 seconds, landed just East of Dover. Bleriot received an ecstatic hero's welcome in London and later in Paris. Latham, true to his promise, made a second attempt on 27th July, but sadly, just 2 miles from Dover, a loose fuel connection forced a second ditching.

All of the events leading up to and during these flights were sensationally reported in the sponsoring *Daily Mail* and also in the wider press, with comprehensive coverage of the participating aircraft. Further detailed technical information was given in *Flight* magazine. Harry's interest was such that when he heard that there was to be a big flying meeting at Rheims in four weeks time he and his friend John Williams made arrangements to be there.

The Rheims Flying Meeting, the world's first such event, brought together the leading aviators and aeroplanes of the day. Most of the aviators were French although Glenn Curtiss the American was there with his biplane and three privately owned Wright 'Flyers' were also present. In all, 15 biplanes and 8 monoplanes were on show. Perhaps due to the recent participation and success of monoplanes in the Channel crossing competition, monoplanes became the focus of Harry's attention, and indeed, they probably would have appeared less complicated and more compact than the biplanes. Of the monoplanes present there were two dominating types, the Bleriot and the Antoinette, and as we will see from Harry's first design, he initially favoured the Bleriot over the Antoinette, although he incorporated aspects of both within his own ideas. The fact that the Bleriot was smaller and required less power than the Antoinette may have been a factor, as Harry would not have wished to take up too much of the J. B. Ferguson workshop space and, with his knowledge of engines, he would have appreciated how limited the power output of the early aero engines was in relation to their weight, a critical factor.

Back home at the end of August both he and John Williams would have been inspired, having actually seen flying machines for the first time, both on the ground and in the air and, with their heads full of ideas and their sketchbooks full of information, their enthusiasm to take part in this new activity must have been tremendous. Of the two, clearly Harry was the one with the greater opportunity to get involved in the practical sense, having the potential backing and the facilities of J. B. Ferguson Ltd. His friend John Williams was undoubtedly fully committed to flying, as was proven later when he joined the Royal Flying

Corps at the outbreak of World War I in 1914, and the Royal Air Force in the Second World War, however it is not thought that his personal circumstances in 1909 would have permitted the same direct commitment as Harry. Nevertheless it is clear that he was very much involved in the design and construction of the machine.

Now Harry, as has been stated, could be extremely convincing and tenacious when he was fully committed to an idea and it probably would not have been all that difficult for him to have persuaded his brother Joe of the potential business opportunities in aviation, however Joe's son, Joe junior, recalled many years later the family understanding that,

'while Joe was over in the States on a business trip Harry got the idea that building and flying a plane would be great publicity for the car company and that when Joe returned two months later he was well into his project...'.

There may well be some truth in this understanding, as it is certainly known that Joe went on an extended business trip to the United States in the Autumn of 1909. It is of interest to know that while in New York he met Wilbur Wright, and while it is likely that it was a fairly casual meeting, they got as far as discussing the use of Irish linen for wing covering and Wilbur confirmed its use on their machines after trying several other fabrics. Wilbur was an extremely impressive man; his direct sincerity and intellect was recognised by all who met him. It would seem likely that Joe would have been similarly impressed and one can see him being more receptive to Harry's aeronautics on his return to Belfast. Whichever way it was, Harry was back home at J.B. Ferguson Ltd. at the beginning of September full of enthusiasm, and it might be thought that he would have started immediately to put his thoughts into action. However this apparently was not the case, as it is known that little more than serious consideration of the possibilities continued until the end of September. The probable reason for this hesitation was the information that there was to be a Salon Aeronautique in Paris from 25th September until 2nd October which would give a further opportunity to study the practicalities of aeroplane design and construction. A

journalist from *Aero* weekly who met Harry at the
Paris Salon reported in the
21st December 1909 issue
of that magazine that he
was convinced of Harry's
serious intentions, but reported him as saying that
no actual drawings for his
machine had yet been started. This situation was confirmed later in their 11th
January 1910 issue, follow-

Lilian Bland at the
controls of her Mayfly
biplane in Lord
O'Neill's deerpark at
Randalstown, where
she made a number
of flights between
September and
December 1910

ing an interview with Harry after his first successful flight, when
Harry stated that his aeroplane had been designed and constructed in 6 weeks.

It is now possible to follow with reasonable certainty the timescale involved in the design and manufacture of Harry's first aeroplane from commencement in early October to the successful
flight at the end of December (see Appendix 6). However before
proceeding with Harry's story, it is interesting to show that he
was not alone in Ulster in taking up flying seriously. There were
at least three other contenders of note in this new enterprise:
Lilian Bland, Joe Cordner and Arthur Blake, and several other
individuals who put considerable effort into flying machines of
one kind or another.

In Carnmoney, just seven miles north of Belfast, a lady of delightful and unusual character and of considerable ability, Miss
Lilian Bland, received a postcard from France in July 1909 showing Bleriot's monoplane, just after his Channel flight. Lilian had
long been interest in bird flight and aroused by the possibility of
getting into the air herself, she started making enquiries through
Flight magazine, requesting help on various aspects of aeroplane
design and construction. In a manner reminiscent of the Wrights
she decided to start with a biplane glider in order to gain experience of the dynamics of flying, with the intention of adding an
engine when that was achieved. Having drafted the basic layout
for a small biplane she went to the Blackpool Flying Meeting on

18th to 25th October, as Harry was also to do, and studied in great detail all the aeroplanes on display. On return she adjusted her plans in accordance with things she had seen and without delay built a 6 ft span biplane glider which flew successfully under tow. Wasting no time she started on a full size version and had this ready to test fly at the end of January 1910, a considerable feat, as she carried out most of the work herself. Over the next four months she flew the 27 ft span glider at Carnmoncy under tow, essentially as a kite, modifying it as the experiments demanded. It proved to be a very strong flier and she confidently ordered a small two-cylinder engine from A. V. Roe. Unfortunately this did not arrive until late July and, although fitted immediately, appalling weather during most of August prevented any trials until the 31st, when on its first run it left the ground and landed safely. She continued these flight trials in the Deerpark at Lord O'Neill's estate in Randalstown over the next 3 to 4 months, making many adjustments to improve her 'Mayfly's' performance. By December she was confident enough to make plans for a larger biplane and early in 1911 she placed an advertisement in *Flight* offering these *'Improved Mayfly'* type aeroplanes for sale *'from £250 without engine'*. However the escalating costs of this enterprise persuaded her to take up her father's offer to buy her a car, from which interest she took out a Ford sub-agency in Belfast. A short time later she married a cousin and emigrated to Canada. Thus ended a remarkable episode, with Lilian Bland entering the record books as the first woman in Ireland, and probably the world, to build and fly an aeroplane of her own design.

In late 1908 Joe Cordner arrived in the city of Londonderry from Lurgan in Co. Armagh and opened up a cycle business similar to the one he had been operating in Lurgan with his twin brother Ted. It will be recalled that Joe Cordner's name has previously been mentioned as a competitor in the first motorcycle race in Ulster at Ballymena in August 1902. Although Joe's education was little more than the basic three Rs, he was intelligent and had a natural mechanical aptitude combined with an enquiring and inventive mind. These talents had led him to engineer various gearing and braking systems for cycles and motorcycles at a time when these machines were relatively new and the market was open for improvements. He had even initiated several patents related to such designs. The sale and repair of cycles and motorcycles provided a reasonable income but Joe was never well off. It may be that his inventive nature saw this new aviation activity as a potential route to greater prosperity, for around the middle of 1909 he started to

Joe Cordner in his first aeroplane on the Lisfannon foreshore near Buncrana in Co. Donegal. Like Harry, he used a JAP engine and a Clarke propeller. His patented wing ducts are clearly shown

plan an aeroplane. There is no information about the source of this inspiration and it is not known whether he visited any of the flying meetings in France or England. It is envisaged that, like Harry, the excitement generated by the Channel flights crystallized a burgeoning interest, and Joe is also likely to have had access to the cycle and motorcar magazines from which he could get illustrations of the most prominent aeroplanes.

His first aeroplane was a very compact monoplane of sound construction, in scale and form rather favouring the Bleriot, but with a tapering, inverted triangular fuselage and non-warping wings supported from a triangular cabane structure. It was however in the control system that Joe introduced a novel concept of his own invention. The undersurfaces of the wings and tail plane were covered with a spanwise series of tapering, V-shaped ducts which were valved by small flaps at the trailing edges where the airflow discharged. From the cockpit these flaps could be opened and closed in groups, either on alternate wings or in unison. The intention was that when operated on alternate wings they would give directional control, while closed in unison they would act as air brakes. There was no rudder at the tail and differential use of the valves on the tailplane ducts was to provide this steering capacity, perhaps in conjunction with the use of the valves on the wings. The aeroplane was transported to Lisfannon near Buncrana in Co. Donegal where there was a long stretch of beach and a level scrubby foreshore. Witnesses have confirmed that, with Joe piloting, the aeroplane did leave the ground, but apparently with little more than short hops being achieved. Despite the

Lisfannon strand being exposed to a main road and railway line, no contemporary accounts of Joe's trial flights were recorded and even their dating is in doubt. It has been stated that they took place in 1908 but this can be ruled out as the engine Joe used, a 35 hp V-8 JAP aero engine exactly similar to that which Harry used, was not available until early 1909. Other undocumented information gives autumn 1909 as the time of these trial flights and if this could be authenticated they would precede Harry's first flight. In the absence of such authentication, which is still being pursued, caution would indicate 1910 or even 1911 as more likely. Joe lodged an application for a patent on his control system in January 1911 and it was granted in September 1911, the illustrations in the application closely following the format of his first aeroplane. Joe had previous experience of the patenting process as he had made several patent applications in connection with cycles and motorcycles while working in Lurgan and he would therefore have been aware of the danger of exposure of an invention prior to the patent being granted. It is thought that this was why he was publicity shy at the time of his trials and the subsequent lack of information on dates. Incidentally, it would seem incredible if Joe had not travelled the short distance from Londonderry to Magilligan to witness Harry's flying activities there in 1910.

From his first trials he seems to have become aware that the control ducts he had designed created considerable drag and that he needed more power to overcome that resistance. He built a second, much modified, version of his first aeroplane. While it retained the original underwing ducts on the mainplanes, the tail now had a fixed tailplane with conventional elevators and a rudder. The main undercarriage was simplified and the machine was fitted with a more powerful French, Anzani radial engine driving a more efficient French, Chauviere propeller. While there would still be reservations about Joe's patented control system, this version looked much more practical. Sadly it was never really put to the test as on its first trial in late 1911 or early 1912, while the engine was being warmed up and before Joe was in the cockpit, it revved up and could not be restrained by Joe and his helpers. Bounding forward it rose and was almost completely destroyed when it crashed into some trees on the field boundary. The expenditure required to rebuild it was beyond Joe's financial situation at that time and, although he experimented with ideas for helicopters for many years afterwards, they only materialized in model form.

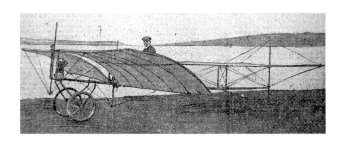

Arthur Blake in the small lightly-framed Bleriot style monoplane he designed and built at Magheramorne near Larne in late 1909. Note large angle of attack of the wings and the tiny single cylinder engine at the nose

In Magheramorne near Larne towards the end of 1909 Arthur V. Blake built a small monoplane of light construction in his garage premises there, where he operated a small motor business, selling and servicing cars and motorcycles. It will be recalled that A. V. Blake took part in the 1906 Muratti Trophy motorcycle trial in which Harry did so well. When other local members of the motor cycling fraternity such as Joe Cordner, Leslie Wilkinson and John Williams are taken into account it emphasises how close the link was between the motor cycling and flying fraternities. The only photograph of Blake's machine yet located, which is fairly heavily touched up, was published in the 20th December 1909 issue of the *Belfast Evening Telegraph*. It shows Mr Blake sitting in the unfinished monoplane. Its basic layout, again rather Bleriot-like, is not unreasonable, as also is its construction although very light. The wire trussed fuselage is uncovered, while the short span, broad chord wings appear to have a single surface covering on well cambered ribs. The tail is not yet complete although there are light tailplane spars and a wire braced rudder post. Well forward there is a simple undercarriage, comprising two heavy bicycle wheels on a plain axle supported by two inverted triangular frames, each fixed to one of the two lower longerons. No propeller is fitted, but there appears to be a very small, single vertical cylinder engine mounted at the front of the fuselage immediately behind a vertical nose strut. The wing chord's angle of attack would seem much too steep for flight as illustrated, but this could have been adjusted following experience during any flight trials, there is however no evidence that this aeroplane was flown or even completed, but it was an intelligent attempt for its time.

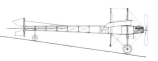

Into the Air

View of Harry
Ferguson's motor
workshop showing
various skilled
craftsmen at work

It is now time to return to J. B. Ferguson's Chichester Street workshops in Belfast in early October 1909.

Harry, with John Williams' help, must have quickly prepared sufficient basic drawings to enable a start to be made. In those days it was rare to draw up elaborate fully detailed drawings from which to work. More usually simple line drawings would have been made showing the general layout and basic dimensions. These would be developed and supplemented by full scale details and part drawings lofted on convenient flat surfaces such as walls, bench tops and even floors, from which the joiners, metal-workers and fitters would work under close direction, as Harry is unlikely to have established all the finer design details right from inception. The *Irish Motor News* of 16th October 1909 reports an interview with Harry who confirms that he had given up his position as Works Manager with J. B. Ferguson Ltd. in order to concentrate on the construction of his new machine. This clearly emphasises his total commitment to the project and his understanding of the need for virtually full-time supervision.

Harry leaning on the
fuselage framework of
his Mark I during its
construction on the
mezzanine floor of
the Chichester Street
worshop, October
1909. Joe Martin
stands second right

Harry was fortunate to have a body of skilled workers available to carry out this work. At that time car manufacturers often supplied their cars to dealers as a fully wheeled and engined chassis, but without bodywork, which would be made to an individual customer's requirements. Thus within the J. B. Ferguson workforce would have been coachbuilders, fitters, metalworkers and upholsterers. It is of interest that it was one of the latter trade, Tom Davison from Drumillar, Dromore who, as an apprentice upholsterer, helped to cover the wings when their framework was complete, while it is known that Willie Evans, a coachbuilder, carried out much of the woodwork.

Harry chose a layout with a long, tapering, rectangular section fuselage and short span, wide chord, square-tipped wings which were to be capable of warping for lateral control. The rather elaborately sprung main wheel undercarriage was to be located far forward close to the engine position. These were all Bleriot style features with the exception of the square wing tips, although the tail configuration was more in the Antoinette fashion, having a 5 ft span triangular tailplane merging with the fuselage sides four bays forward from the rudder post, with a truncated triangular elevator and split trapezoidal rudders. Each wing of 16 ft span and 6 ft parallel chord was constructed around five relatively light spars springing from a solid rib member at the wing root. The aerofoil section of the wings was formed by light ribs spanning chordwise over and under the five spars between the leading and trailing edge trims. Two of the spars on each wing were stiffened by king-post systems. The wings were connected to each other and attached to the fuselage by two substantial bearers fixed to the solid ribs at each wing root and positioned to leave the wing leading edge about 3" below top longeron level and leaving 6" gaps between the wing roots and the fuselage on each side. A triangular cabane pylon, which extended down to carry the main undercarriage was fixed to the fuselage near the leading edges of the wings, provided anchorage for the flying and landing wires. An under-fuselage pylon located near the wing trailing edge carried the wing warping cables. From the under-fuselage pylon back to the tail the construction was in the form of a light timber framework trussed by tensioned wire bracings, while the structure forward of this was formed mainly from light steel components similarly braced. The pylons and undercarriage members used light tubular steel members. The wings were constructed entirely from American elm, covered with a new aeroplane cloth produced by the Dunlop Rubber Company.

An early decision had to be made regarding the choice of engine, a choice that was very limited at that time. Essentially such aero engines were based on automobile or marine engine designs, but modified to reduce weight and maximize output in order to provide the higher power to weight ratio required by the on the limit aerodynamics of that time. Harry had calculated that he required an engine in the 30-35hp range and had seen such an engine at the Paris Salon in September. This was the British-made Green engine; a water cooled engine with 4 upright cylinders, weighing 158 lbs. The Green engine was the best known of the few British aero engines then available and so it was a logical choice. It was normally supplied with a heavy external flywheel fitted to the end of the crankshaft as a precaution against crankshaft vibration arising from misfiring or propeller flutter and generally to maintain the regular momentum of the engine. The flywheel was sometimes omitted to give a weight saving of 23½ lbs.

It was in this latter state that the Green engine was delivered to Harry. The engine was very much his province and, keen to get on with his preparations, he immediately had it bench-mounted to test its performance. As there was no propeller available to offer any balancing

First trial mating of wings and fuselage of Harry's first aeroplane on the ground floor motor showroom in Chichester Street in October 1909. Note the five spar wings. Harry is seated on the wheel of the as-yet uncompleted undercarriage, while his construction team stand beside the rear fuselage

resistance he decided that a flywheel would be needed and he rigged up a temporary one using an old brass bound pulley wheel fitted to the crankshaft extension.

Unfortunately it proved even more temporary than expected, for as soon as the engine fired it disintegrated spectacularly, scattering pieces and admiring workers in all directions and severely damaging the overrunning engine. Fortunately none of the expectant observers was injured. Harry was forced to abandon this damaged engine, at a loss incidentally of £365 (c. £30,000 today), and to consider an alternative. The Green engine was water cooled and as such incurred the added weight and complication of a radiator and its associated coolant water system. This factor is likely to have influenced Harry in his next choice, a 30-35 hp V8, air cooled engine weighing 187 lbs, a product of Messrs J. A. Prestwich. This firm had produced successful motorcycle engines for several years and their products would therefore have been known to Harry. They had recently moved to fill the gap in the aero engine market and fortunately could supply this suitably sized engine with almost immediate delivery. Their engines were commonly referred to as JAP engines, which could lead to confusions of source outside the engineering trade and those who used them, sometimes being described as Japanese engines!

Between 18th and 25th October, halfway into the final construction period of Harry's first aeroplane, there was a Flying Meeting at Blackpool which Harry attended, accompanied by John Williams. During this brief interlude away from the workshop at Blackpool he would have had the opportunity to see at least one JAP engine on display, albeit of lower horsepower, and this may also have influenced his second choice of engine.

While he was away at Blackpool he fortunately had the able back-up of John McKee who had returned to J. B. Ferguson Ltd. in 1907 and this enabled the construction of his aeroplane to continue during his absence, indeed it is thought that McKee contributed a lot of practical help during the whole process.

The next problem for Harry was the choice of propeller. This was a vital piece of equipment, as no matter how efficient the aero engine might be, any power generated needed to be convert- ed effectively into thrust by the propeller. Although the Wright Brothers as early as 1903 had brilliantly worked out the design principles associated with propellers, this information was not generally available and in England and France even as late as 1909, and very few of the selection available on the market there were truly scientifically designed or particularly efficient.

In England at that time four manufacturers prominently adver- tised their propellers, Cochrane, Beedle, Clarke and Handley- Page, while a few French Chauviere propellers were starting to be imported. The Cochrane propeller had light corrugated steel or aluminium blades, joined together by steel leading edges which were reinforced where they joined the engine drive shaft. The Beedle propellers had very unusual scimitar-shaped sheet metal blades carried on a slender steel arm, strengthened at the drive shaft location. The Clarke propellers were made of carefully shaped timber, the form that would soon become the standard construction for propellers, and the Handley-Page propellers were of similar construction but this firm was not a specialist propeller manufacturer. Initially Harry chose the Beedle propel- ler, and it was used on his first flight trials.

Towards the end of October the JAP engine arrived and enabled the front of the fuselage framework with its engine bearers to be completed and the engine installed.

In early November, in anticipation of his aeroplane's completion, Harry started his search for a suitable flying ground. The relatively small size and shape of the fields on the Ferguson farm ruled out this obvious choice, indeed this small field size was typical of most Ulster farms in those days and so a more spacious location needed to be identified. It became clear that the most suitable locations would be found within the large demesnes of the aristocracy of landed gentry. The Hillsborough Demesne of the Downshire Family was just 4 miles from the Ferguson farm at Growell, and the Downshire land agent and his farm workers would have known the Fergusons well. It is also thought that the Downshires or their Land Agent acquired cars through J. B. Ferguson Ltd., making it likely that Harry would have helped to service them at Hillsborough, in the same way that he had visited the Greer household in Cookstown to maintain their cars and had impressed them with his ability and character. These various connections are the likely source of his being able to gain permission to use the Hillsborough Large Park for his first trials.

On or about 16th November his first aeroplane was complete and he immediately had it transported to Hillsborough, towed behind a car on its main wheels with its wings stowed on either side of the fuselage. For clarity of reference to the subsequent variants of his aeroplane this one is classified as the Ferguson Mark 1, and is illustrated on drawing no 1.

November is clearly not an ideal time of year for flight trials, especially in those days when aviators, even in summer, very often had to restrict themselves to early morning or early evening for flights, when the wind forces tended to be less. But Harry was more impatient than ever as he had set himself the target of flying before the year was out. Some idea of the strength of this inner driving force and his ability to bring others along with him can be imagined when studying the contemporary photographs showing the exposed terrain, sometimes snow covered, and think about the proper setting up of the aeroplane in its entirety for the first time, with its steel rigging and control wires, and working on the cold metal of the engine, all the time without any shelter from the November winds. Harry himself is seen seated in a perilously exposed position, half out of the open framed fuselage,

The Mark I in Hillsborough Large Park soon after arrival in November 1909. Harry is in the cockpit, Leslie Wilkinson is on the mainwheel and Joe Martin is at the wingtip on the right. Note complicated undercarriage and stiffener across the face of the Beedle propeller blades. The Beedle proved ineffective and seems to have been easily damaged

apparently in a lounge suit with shirt and tie, bareheaded and without goggles or gloves, or any kind of safety harness.

Fitted with the strange Beedle propeller he made a number of trial runs across the open parkland over the next few days as weather permitted. On a few occasions the aeroplane hopped off the ground but never seriously seemed to be anxious to fly. There was no shelter to accommodate the aeroplane at night or during inclement weather. Fortunately the wings and the tail surfaces were covered with a rubberised Dunlop fabric that had good weathering properties and, with a tarpaulin over the engine, the machine survived the week long trials, requiring little more than minor repairs to the undercarriage, adjustments to the rigging wires and some engine tuning. However as the trials progressed it became clear to Harry that in its present set up his aeroplane was not capable of true flight, and at the end of the week he had it transported back to the workshop for modifications.

During the next two weeks Harry modified the machine, based on his initial experience in Hillsborough. In order to reduce weight he simplified the main undercarriage by removing the original springing mechanism with its supporting struts and associated curved central skid. He also decided to change the wings. When he had been at the Blackpool Flying Meeting he had again been impressed by the Antoinette monoplane in which Latham had made a successful flight in near gale conditions. He was particularly interested in that machine's wing layout, as on return to Belfast he wrote off to *Flight* magazine for any available details on the Antoinette, with particular reference to its tapered wings.

At the time he contacted *Flight* the parallel chord

The Mark IA with tapered wings, additional upper pylon and simplified undercarriage in Hillsborough Large Park, December 1909. Harry stands to the right of the propeller and Leslie Wilkinson to the left. The external propeller blade stiffener, as seen on the Mark I photo, is not fitted.

wings of his first aeroplane were already under construction and he had used these wings during his first trials, but when he returned to Hillsborough a set of slightly tapered wings had been installed. It is not certain whether these were modified versions of the original wings or completely new ones. If the latter case, it would seem unlikely that they could have been completed during the two week period between the two sets of trials, and he would have needed to have organized the construction of this spare set shortly after his Blackpool visit. The new wings were of similar span, but the width of the wing roots was increased to 6ft 6in and the tips reduced to 5ft 6in. The five spar wing construction and king-post stiffenings were retained. The original parallel chord wings had been supported from a single inverted V cabane pylon which seems not to have given sufficient coverage, as an additional inverted V pylon was now fitted in front of the cockpit and directly over the V pylon under the fuselage, to which the rear flying wires were attached and through which the wing warping cables operated. The new wings were positioned approximately 8" further back on the fuselage but with much the same dihedral and angle of attack. This may have been related to the repositioning of the main undercarriage wheels approximately 1 foot to the rear, where they were now fixed directly to the bottom of the front pylon members. The tailplanes, elevator and split rudders were unchanged.

It is known that during the initial trials the strange Beedle propeller had not satisfied Harry, and had proved susceptible to damage, one photograph showing an additional stiffening member fitted across the blades, while its pulling power was in doubt, which is not surprising considering its strange format. Harry had therefore ordered a Cochrane propeller, but this cannot have

This rear view of the Mark 1A in Hillsborough Large Park in December 1909 shows clearly the pilot's position with the two control wheels, and the tapered wings with their king-post strengthening systems. The man behind the tail is holding a Beedle propeller, either before fitting, or after some damage. Harry, near the cockpit, is – as usual – dressed in a lounge suit, collar and tie despite the winter weather

been delivered by 13th December, for he started the second trials at Hillsborough on the Ferguson Mark 1A, still using the Beedle propeller. The Mark 1A layout is shown in drawing 2 in the appendices.

It was now mid December: he had to struggle against weather delays, while constantly making adjustments to the rigging and the engine. It must also be remembered that Harry had never been at the controls of a moving aeroplane before his own first trials in late November and even then he had experienced little more than a few short hops, which could hardly be considered true flying experience. For the first few days while still using the Beedle propeller little improvement seemed to have been made and the Large Park now had a light covering of snow. Around about 18th or 20th December the Cochrane propeller arrived and was immediately fitted. Although this propeller too was not a conventional one in the modern sense, it was clearly more efficient than the Beedle and the machine was propelled across the snow-covered ground more rapidly than before. Although very short hops, or jumps caused by uneven ground conditions were still the order of the day, there were signs of greater lift being generated. There are indications that the wing incidence was being adjusted as the trials proceeded, which also may have contributed to the improvement.

Two valuable days were lost to Christmas Day and Boxing Day, Saturday and Sunday 25th and 26th December and time was

running out on Harry's self-imposed deadline.

Until this time most of the trial runs had been made across the slightly more level part of the Park. In an effort to attain more speed over the ground and generate greater lift it was decided to move to a downward sloping part of the Park for the next trial runs. Almost immediately there were signs of improvement although the wind was blustery and Harry had great difficulty in keeping control in the brief times the machine was off the ground. Friday 31st December was again cold and the wind was gusting between 25 and 30 mph, but Harry was determined to prove his aeroplane could fly and this was going to be the day. After some encouraging short runs he had the machine taken further back up the slope and on the next descent the machine skimmed just above the ground for about 50 yards. Harry was not satisfied that this effort was really a proper flight and despite a freshening wind he took the machine right to the top of the incline and readied it for a further attempt. This time the machine lifted off almost immediately and flew for approximately 130 yards, at a maximum height of about 15 ft above the ground. Success at last – or at least for the time being – as Harry knew in his heart that there was some way to go before he would be flying confidently and consistently under full control, but he had achieved his first goal of making the first flight in Ireland by an Irishman in an Irish aeroplane, and before the end of 1909.

Three recorded reports of Harry's flying success on Friday 31st

This is the only known photograph of the Mark IA in motion and off the ground at Hillsborough in December 1909, although it does not record the first historic flight. The long, slender and rather fragile fuselage is clearly shown. Although indistinct, the propeller is probably a Cochrane, as this was used when the first flight was made.

December 1909 are included below as perhaps the best way of covering this first milestone of Harry's flying enterprise. The first is by a *Belfast Telegraph* reporter who witnessed the flight. The second report in *Flight* magazine of 8th January 1910 is clearly based on contact with Harry but is a journalistic report of the event with some of the background detail leading up to it and some technical information on the machine itself. The third is a report from the *Aero* magazine of 11th January 1910 based on a communication from Harry and quoting some of his own descriptions.

Belfast Telegraph: 'The exhaust is a perfectly free one and without a silencer of any kind, so that the roar of the eight cylinders was like the sound of a Gatling gun in action. The machine was set against the wind, and all force being developed, the splendid pull of the new propeller swept the big aeroplane along as Mr Ferguson advanced the lever. Presently, at the movement of the pedal, the aeroplane rose in the air to a height from nine to twelve feet, amidst the hearty cheers of the onlookers. The poise of the machine was perfect, and Mr Ferguson made a splendid flight of 130 yards. Although fierce gusts of wind made the machine wobble a little twice, the navigator steadied her by bringing her head to wind. Then he brought the machine to earth safely after having accomplished probably the most successful initial flight that has ever been attempted in an aeroplane'.

Flight Magazine: 'The Emerald Isle is not by any means far behind the times in matters of practical value, and among the several flying machines which have been built and experimented with, that of Mr H.G. Ferguson, of Belfast, appears to give very good promise of success. So far the work of trying it out has been hampered by the lack of a suitable ground, but it is hoped that this will shortly be remedied. It has been located at Lord Downshire's park at Hillsborough, but this, having proved to be too hilly, a move has been decided upon. During the three weeks the monoplane has been at Hillsborough, the weather has been all against practice, but on the last day of the old year Mr Ferguson, after fitting a new Cochrane propeller, was successful in getting the machine to rise and fly for 130 yards, and this in spite of a gusty wind blowing at an average rate of 25 miles per hour. During this trial Mr

Ferguson had the machine under perfect control and landed again without difficulty. The machine is a monoplane somewhat suggestive of the Bleriot cross-channel flyer, having a supporting surface of 192 sq. ft, the main planes being 34 ft span. They are mounted with a dihedral of 4 deg., while the angle of incidence when flying is 7 deg. The length of the machine is 30 ft and the weight is 620 lbs. It is fitted with a 7 ft tractor, driven at a speed of 1,2000 revs. per min. by a 35 hp 8-cyl, air-cooled JAP engine, and a speed of 32 miles has to be obtained before lifting is accomplished. The monoplane was constructed entirely in the works of Messrs J. B. Ferguson Ltd, of Belfast and was designed by Mr H.G. Ferguson after studying the various aeroplanes which took part in the Rheims and Blackpool meetings. The owner hopes to be the first to fly across the Irish Channel, and moreover to accomplish it before long'.

Aero Magazine: 'Mr H. G. Ferguson, the first man to fly in Ireland, writes us that on December 31st he made a most successful clear flight of 100 yards. This may be reckoned as the first actual flight, his other attempts being only sufficient to prove that the machine could leave the ground. This was performed by the aid of a Cochrane propeller. Nothing further will be attempted for a few days, for he intends to change his flying ground, as the present one is very bad. Mr Ferguson gives a modest but graphic account of his flight, from which we give the following extracts;

"The wind was blowing at a speed of about twenty eight miles per hour and, of course, to go out with the machine was foolishness, but I dearly wanted to make a flight worth mentioning in the papers before 1910 came in, and this is the only excuse I can offer. Before attempting anything worth publishing I made about a dozen trials and got clear of the ground every time for about twenty yards, but then had to switch off owing to there being no room for me to go further. I then took the machine up a long incline, which was the only way I could fly into the wind, and made one very successful flight of about fifty yards down this against the wind; then, as the wind seemed to be getting worse, I determined to make a bold bid before it did so, and I took the machine up to the very top of the hill. Wilkinson started the engine for me, and when I got it opened full out and running at great speed I waved the chaps behind to let go. This they did, and before I had gone

seven yards (I measured the distance) the machine was clear of
the ground and I was flying. I kept it rising for about 100 yards, and
was then about 15 ft high. Owing to the speed of the wind I was
not travelling at speed of more than ten miles an hour, which represents a fairly long flight in the air. The land all about where I was
going down is awfully hilly, and suddenly a gust struck the machine
on the left wing, tipping her up almost perpendicularly. I warped
the right wing and brought her back again. When she was almost
straight an even worse gust caught her and threw her straight up
on to the right wing; the very outside edge was struck into the
ground and brought the side of the wings round into the wind".

This, of course, brought the flight to an abrupt conclusion, but
neither the machine nor Mr Ferguson was hurt in any way. Mr
Ferguson continues; "You may guess how strong the wind was
when during the 100 yards all the chaps said that the machine actually stopped in the air and was moved backwards. Of course,
as I said before, I would not have though of risking the machine
for one moment on such a day as yesterday, only I wanted to
be in the same year as flying has really been made successful".

The monoplane was designed and constructed entirely in the
works of J.B. Ferguson Ltd, Belfast. Its dimensions and main particulars are as follows: Spread of the planes, 34 ft; length, 30 ft;
dihedral angle, 4 deg.; flying angle of incidence, 7 deg.; supporting surface, 192 sq.ft; weight, 620 lbs; weight per sq.ft
of supporting surface, 3.22 lbs.; Cochrane tractor, 7 ft diam.;
speed of tractor, 1,200 rpm; lifting speed of machine, 32
miles per hour; engine, 35 hp air cooled eight cylinder JAP.

The machine is being removed from Lord Downshire's
park at Hillsborough to a more suitable flying ground,
as the former place as proved much too hilly.

"Our congratulations to Mr Ferguson on his pluck and perseverance, and especially on the concentration of en-
ergy which enabled him to build and fly a machine all inside six weeks. Compare this with some of the would-be
leaders of 'aviation' in this country, who have been building machines for years, and still show no signs of flying.'

The exact location of Harry's first flight within the 1000 acres of Hillsborough Large Park has exercised those with an in-depth interest in Ireland's aviation history for many years. In Appendix 7 the writer gives an assessment of the little contemporary information available on this aspect of the flight trials there, together with a study of the site as it is today, and puts forward a reasoned view for the location.

The Ups
and Downs of Flying

The Mark 1B at Masserene in transition to 1C standard. The underwing protective hoops have been omitted, the rear fuselage is covered and a tailfin has been added. The Clarke propeller has been fitted

Flushed with his success on 31ˢᵗ December 1909, Harry was full of enthusiasm to continue his flying activities but knew that his aeroplane needed further modifications to improve its flying capacity and in January he started out on a process of development that extended right through the year until October, continuously modifying its configuration and its detail as and when flying it indicated weaknesses or suggested opportunities for improvement. As will be seen very considerable effort was involved in this enterprise and it would seem unlikely that he would be contributing much to the J. B. Ferguson motor business during the year, other than the spin-off publicity that his pioneering flying activities would generate.

Harry had been reasonably satisfied with the modified wings he had used on the Mark 1A when he achieved his first flight at Hillsborough and he proposed to continue with them at least initially on his next flight trials. However he considered that wings of greater area could give improved performance and the construction of a new set of wings of increased span was initiated. There was still some concern regarding the effectiveness of the rear sets of wing support

Harry seated in the Mark 1B at Masserene in early February 1910. A good view is given of the control wheel that operated the wing warping cables. In later versions this was changed to a more direct operating control lever

wires, despite the previous addition of a second upper pylon on the Mark 1A. Accordingly, the upper and lower rear pylons were now repositioned half a bay towards the tail, giving greater support coverage to the wings. Other modifications were also carried out. The rear fuselage from the leading points of the tailplane to the rudder post was now covered in fabric and a triangular fabric tailfin was added to the top of the fuselage over the same length of fuselage. The tailwheel was simplified to an unsprung vertical bicycle fork with light side braces and moved back to the last fuselage frame before the rudder post. The pilot's controls in the form of two hand wheels and two foot pedals were retained. In this form his aeroplane is designated as Mark 1B. As the changes involved are visually minor and were retained on the next version, drawing no 3 may be used to cover both.

Harry had not been satisfied with the undulating and hilly terrain at Hillsborough and had been searching for an alternative flying ground. Lord Antrim offered him the use of Masserene park near Antrim Town and having inspected it he thought that it might be suitable, although as will be seen, following a series of trials with both sets of wings he was later forced to look elsewhere. Masserene Park, on the shore of Lough Neagh was typical parkland with large plantations enclosing open ground dotted with clumps of trees, but there seemed to be sufficient clear spaces within it for his purposes and it had the merits of being fairly

Group of Automobile
Association members
in front of the Mark
1C at Masserene in
April 1910. On Harry's
right is John Brown of
Dunmurry, the first
motor car owner in
Ireland, and to his left,
J.C. Percy and Francis
Wilde, the assistant
secretary of the AA.
Note the machine's
increased wingspan,
heightened main
undercarriage and
the Clarke propeller

level and of being well away from any high ground that might produce downdraughts.

Although the Cochrane propeller had enabled Harry to make his first flight at Hillsborough he was still far from satisfied with its performance and he had ordered an Integrale propeller from the French manufacturer, Chauviere, and another from the English manufacturer, T. W. K. Clarke & Co., both of whose products were highly rated. There is no certain evidence that an Integrale was ever used and Harry recorded no specific comments on it, but there is one photo of the Mark 1B which shows it with a propeller that appears to have a more rounded shape than the Clarke product and this may be an Integrale.

In early February while waiting for the new wings he tried out the Mark 1B at the new flying ground at Masserene Park and had some limited success, with numerous short hops and brief flights, but during these trials he found, as will be described more fully later, that the grass at Masserene was longer than he had realised and concealed numerous ruts. As the Clarke propeller he was awaiting was to have a greater 7'0" diameter he decided to increase the height of the main undercarriage by about 10", to give better ground clearance.

The Clarke propeller had now arrived, and when the new wings came on site in early April they were fitted immediately. They each tapered from 7'0" at the root to 5'0" at the tip and were based on two spars rather than the five spars used previously. Although the two spars were of slightly increased girth, overall there should be a reduction in weight, compensating for the additional four ribs on each wing and the associated additional area of fabric covering. The overall span of the new wings was approximately 40'0", which was 6'0" greater than the original wings. This increased span would more than ever require stiffening and the king-post systems were therefore retained. The original under-wing protective hoops were omitted, but a small horn was fitted to the leading edge at each wingtip. The petrol tank was repositioned approximately 6" forward. On a less practical note, in true Harry Ferguson style, he emblazoned the nose of the machine with a very large version of the newly established Automobile Association's AA sign, clearly acquired through the J. B. Ferguson Ltd. motor trade connection, perhaps another little publicity plug and a placatory nod to his brother Joe, who was yet to be fully convinced of the value of Harry's aeronautical activities. In this Mark 1C form, as illustrated on drawing No 3, he continued his flight trials into May with many further short hops and at least one flight of about a mile. One plus from these trials was the convincing performance of the Clarke propeller.

While at Masserene Harry contributed to the creation of another Irish flying record, although not quite up to the standard created by his first flight at Hillsborough! For part of the time that Harry was at Masserene, a party of Boy Scouts from the 15th Belfast Troop had been camping there. Noting their interest in his activities he gave short flights to two of them, J. L. Tegart and F. R. Allen, ensuring that their names would go down in the history of Scouting as the first Boy Scouts in Ireland and perhaps in Great Britain, to fly in an aeroplane.

It must be appreciated that Harry's ability to improve his piloting skills was limited by the brief times he was able to remain airborne and the restriction on aerial manoeuvres caused by the space limitations of the Park, with little more than straight line flights being possible. The machine's controls were still far from precise and executing turns required more space than was available, while flying over banks of trees was not yet an option.

During his time at Masserene he was visited by a group of members from the growing Automobile Association, of which he had recently become a member. Accompanying them was Belfast born J. C. Percy, whose name has appeared previously in this account in connection with the early motoring trials in which Harry had participated. He had also been a prime mover in the formation of the Aero Club and had embraced aviation with great enthusiasm. The party observed the limitations of the Masserene location and J. C. Percy, who was also editor of the *Motor News,* recorded his impressions of Harry's activities and his difficulties there in that magazine;

'The grass is long, the surface rough and full of ruts, while a wire fencing on one side and Lough Neagh on the other 'cribs and confines' his best efforts. An elephant would just have as much chance of playing leap frog in his cage at the Zoo as Mr Ferguson would in doing brilliant aviation feats inside the limits of his present arena … To start with, therefore, Mr Ferguson is very seriously handicapped in his experimental work. Above and beyond everything else, the aviator wants room. Take Mr Ferguson's machine, for example. It requires a run of 300 yards before the lifting point is reached, and getting such a run over the coarse, rough grass of Masserene Park is impossible.

Notwithstanding this drawback, Mr Ferguson has made remarkable progress. Nearly every day he is able to get a short fly – I say short flight, because the limitations of the ground makes an extended aerial tour dangerous … The day chosen to observe Mr Ferguson's trials following an invitation by him, proved to be the worst so far in the month of April. The wind was blowing at a rate of thirty miles per hour, and to be perfectly candid, when I found the condition of affairs prevailing, I did not encourage my young friend to carry out his promise. He was not to be put off, however. I had come from Dublin to see him fly, and he was not going to send me back without an ocular demonstration as to the capabilities of his machine. At the same time, he pointed out that there was just a doubt that he might not be able to come down as gently as a bird. Well, I took my place along with Mr Murray, a well known

motorist from Newcastle, Co. Down, in the centre of the field, the
starting place being on the edge of the lough. Mr Ferguson select-
ed our grand stand with the object of flying past us. I was simply
amazed at the ease with which the engine started. Two turns of
the engine and off she went. What a contrast to the long delays
on starting we experienced at Blackpool. The plucky young aviator then took his seat and steered straight for our party. Gradually
we watched the graceful monoplane rise from the ground, first
a few inches, then a few feet, but she was making straight for the
spectators. At first I thought it was a joke. As the machine got
nearer I could see that the wind was too strong, and the machine
did not respond to the tiller, so with that self-preservation which
is the first law of nature, we all ran like redshanks and only just
had time to get clear when the aeroplane swept over the ground
we had been standing on. This demonstration was short, sharp,
but decisive. It was carried out with a following wind of great velocity, but it abundantly proved that Ferguson could not only get
into the air, but was able to control the machine when there. The
next trial was even more successful. At the second time of ask-
ing he got away with even more ease. On this occasion he got up
and flew for over 100 yards, reaching an altitude of about 15 to
20 ft. The descent, however, was not quite so successful, as a gust
of wind made landing almost impossible. He reached the ground,
however, with no more serious mishap than a broken wheel.'

J.C. Percy was so convinced of the importance of Harry's aeronautical developments and his need of access to more suitable
flying locations that, using his prestige within the motoring and
sporting fraternities, he tried to obtain the use of either of the
two race tracks at Phoenix Park, Dublin or the Curragh in Co.
Kildare. He also tried to interest the British Secretary of War, the
Right Hon. R.B. Haldane, in making the government's facilities
at the Curragh available. None of these overtures proved successful. Fortunately for Harry's continued progress however, Mr
George Leeke of the Bellarena Rural District Council in County
Londonderry heard of Harry's difficulty and suggested to him
that the strands at Magilligan Point would be the ideal location
for such activities, giving as they did uninterrupted beaches on
either side of the peninsula, each approximately 5 miles long,
and providing extensive space at low tide. Harry lost no time in

making a thorough inspection of the area and quickly decided to move there for his further trials. Before proceeding there however, he decided on further modifications to his aeroplane based on the knowledge gained even in his limited time at Masserene.

During the brief flight trials there he had realised that the fabric enclosure of the rear fuselage, open at its front end and closed at the rudder post, added greatly to the aircraft's drag and this was removed. However the front fuselage sides from behind the engine bay to one bay behind the cockpit were now canvas covered. The triangular fabric tailfin was retained however, and the top rudder was enlarged into a truncated triangular shape, while the elevator was made fully triangular and adjusted to fit the span of the tailplane which had been increased to 6 ft. The fuselage was lengthened by about 18 inches at the nose. Harry considered the larger span wings of the Mark 1C had been of doubtful advantage, the additional drag and weight on his low powered machine outweighing any increased lift. Accordingly he reverted to shorter span wings by taking approximately 3 ft from the tips of each of the two-spar wings. This reduction of span permitted the omission of the king-post systems, a welcome simplification. The leading edges of the wings were moved forward approximately 16 inches, thus more or less retaining their position in relation to the lengthened nose. As before the wing spars and edge trims were housed into the substantial wing root members, but the leading one of the two wing connecting bearers now spanned over the top longerons leaving the wing leading edge approximately 6" higher than before. The angle of incidence was reduced to about 5 degrees, which resulted in the wing being much higher up on the fuselage. The space of about 6" between the top longerons and the wing roots was retained. Once again the cabane pylons were changed. The front one with its associated main wheels remained in its original position, although with the lengthened engine bay it was now further back from the aircraft's nose. Not only was the additional main undercarriage height of the Mark 1C retained, but the mainwheel spars rising to form the front pylon were also lengthened above top longeron level, making it 6" to 8" higher. The rear pylon was returned half a bay forward to its earlier location and increased in height to match the front pylon. The under fuselage pylon was moved into line with its upper counterpart and the two main undercarriage stays were lengthened to connect with the bottom longerons at this rear pylon position. These changes placed the pylons and the associated undercarriage structure in line with the two wing spars and at greater distances above and below them, the increased angles improving the effectiveness of the flying and landing wires. The cockpit, previously located in the second fuse-lage bay behind the rear pylon, was now repositioned in the bay immediately behind that pylon, with the rudimentary passen-ger's position remaining between the pylons. Although the wing trailing edges now overlapped the pilots position, the 6" wing root clearances from the fuselage gave sufficient space to operate the wing warping and elevator controls positioned externally at the pilot's left and right hands. The wing warping wheel on the left hand side of the fuselage however, was now changed to a le-ver, with the other controls remaining as before. The cylindrical petrol tank, previously at high level, was now suspended beneath the fuselage just behind the engine. By the first week in June all these modifications were complete and Harry prepared to send his Mark 1D version to his new flying ground. Drawing No 4 il-lustrates the Mark 1D version.

The Magilligan peninsula is triangular in shape, projecting 4½ miles into Lough Foyle from the 1300 ft high Binevenagh es-carpment towards Greencastle on the Donegal shore, creating a 1 mile wide narrows between Lough Foyle and the open Atlantic. The north eastern side of the peninsula is bounded by the 5 mile long Magilligan strand, while on the north western side there is the Foyle or back strand of similar length. The Magilligan strand, or beach, averages approximately 150 yards wide at low tide, while in the same condition the back strand is about 600 yards wide near the Point, increasing to around 1¼ miles wide towards Bellarena. Both beaches have relatively shallow gradients from which the tide recedes, revealing extensive firm and unobstruct-ed surfaces of fine sand. Both strands are backed by sandhills reaching a maximum of 40 ft above sea level on the Magilligan side but rarely more than 25 ft high on the Foyle side; indeed the great majority of the peninsula, essentially an ancient sand-bar, never rises much more than 30 ft above sea level. In 1910 the western half of the peninsula accommodated rather treeless

farmlands, with the eastern half largely scrub land and sandhills. With the flat nature of the land and its exposure to the west and to the north east, there is little protection from strong winds. Bearing in mind the lightness of early aeroplanes and their limited controls this was likely to limit flying hours, but the relative lowness of the sandhills along the beaches should reduce downdraughts, with gusting perhaps the main concern. Out at the Point at that time there was the Napoleonic Martello Tower, the three storey Point Hotel, a licensed bar, a small single storey Isolation Hospital for infectious diseases, and little else. An open-boat ferry linked Magilligan and Greencastle on an irregular basis, weather and tides permitting. Today the fine Martello Tower and the licensed bar, now a fully licensed restaurant, are all that remain of the 1910 period and to these have been added a few discreetly designed modern houses and a less than impressive car-ferry terminal. Two nearby military firing ranges and a large civilian prison located approximately 1½ miles away along the only public road contribute to a rather restrictive atmosphere, perhaps a little like the remote feel the Point area would have had in 1910. Fortunately the distant outlook in all directions is very fine and the magnificent Magilligan, or Benone, beach is easily reached and well serviced at its eastern end, while most of the farmland at the south west of the peninsula remains much as it was back then. See Appendix 8.

On Saturday 9th June 1910 the components of this Mark 1D machine were dispatched to Magilligan by rail and arrived at Bellarena station just after midday. They were taken by cart to Magilligan Point and unloaded in a hollow in the sandhills just off the beach near the Point Hotel where Harry had arranged to make his base and, such

The Mark 1D being assembled on the back strand at Magilligan Point on arrival from Masserene on 9th June 1910. Harry at right supervising

was his enthusiasm, that a start was immediately made on its erection and by seven o'clock the machine was ready to fly. He had it manhandled the short distance out on to the beach over the track used by local fishermen just below the licenced Point Bar and the engine was started up. Unfortunately his enthusiasm was frustrated by a stiff northerly breeze and he was prevented from doing anything more than fast taxiing runs, although these enabled him to get the feel of the machine on the sandy surface and to experience the amount of space available at low tide.

One local journalist mentions the use of a hangar near the Hotel. It is quite likely that Harry had a small timber-framed shed erected convenient to the beach, as it was an exposed area and some work for the machine could only be done satisfactorily under cover. The use of the word hangar, which would not yet have been common, seems to suggest that the journalist heard Harry or one of his colleagues using that term, thus confirming its existence.

The weather remained unsuitable on Sunday, but on Monday morning it was sufficiently improved to allow Harry to execute several short low flights along Magilligan strand and on one of these flights Harry carried a passenger. By evening a large number of onlookers had arrived to experience this novel activity. Fortunately Harry was able to please them with a brief flight before the weather deteriorated again and further flights became impossible.

On Tuesday 12th June conditions were still against flying, but the opportunity was taken to enclose the front part of the fuselage in an effort to reduce the aeroplane's air resistance. The Dunlop rubberised fabric that covered the wings was again used.

Very early in the morning of Wednesday 12th, at around 4 am, Harry made a flight of about 1 mile along Magilligan strand and so, by the afternoon, a large crowd of spectators had gathered expectantly to witness events, despite the threat of a thunderstorm, and they were rewarded by a flight of about 2½ miles at 30-40 ft above the back strand towards Bellarena. On the return flight to the Point he had to descend rather abruptly due to engine trouble, slightly buckling a wheel in the landing, preventing further flights that day. Until 24th June, Harry had his machine out as often as the weather permitted using whichever beach was most suitable for flying, although the wider expanse of the back strand at low tide was the most practical. He was reasonably satisfied with the make-up of the aeroplane, although he had now accepted that the 35 hp JAP engine was not really powerful enough, as the small margin between staying airborne and being forced to descend had been amply demonstrated in the often gusty conditions at Magilligan. On 25th Harry became quite ill and had to abandon further flying until 9th July, when he arrived back at Magilligan to take up where he had left off.

News of his return having spread widely throughout the area, a crowd estimated at well over 2,000 assembled at Magilligan on Sunday 10th July to witness the proceedings, swamping the limited capacity of the Point Hotel and such little other facilities on offer in this remote area. Fortunately it was a beautiful day, making the long wait for the aviator to perform quite pleasurable and spiced with expectancy. The dozens of motor cars and other vehicles arriving and taking up positions on the strand was in itself at that time quite a spectacle, while the hundreds of bicycles wheeling about added to the general excitement. At 6 pm Harry ordered his machine to be taken down on to the west back strand and started preparations to fly, by which time all vantage points in the sand hills and on the shore were filled with spectators. Harry climbed into the cockpit and on his order the propeller was swung and the engine broke loudly into life. He revved up the unsilenced engine, further impressing the crowd and, when satisfied with its steady running, instructed his helpers to release the aircraft, which quickly gathered speed, lifted off and ascended to a height of about 35 ft. He flew steadily at this height over the strand for ¾ mile towards Bellarena and then turned in a wide sweep out over Lough Foyle for perhaps ½ mile before turning back towards the shoreline to return to base. While still above the tide he was hit by a sudden gust forcing the machine right down to the surface of the water. As he fought to regain control the wheels and the propeller tips actually touched the water showering him with spray and had his engine not kept going there is no doubt he would have crashed into the sea. As it was he was able to coax the machine into a gentle climb and gain enough height to enable him to reach the shore and make a safe landing. Needless to say the crowd were delighted with this thrilling incident and Harry's skillful recovery, and applauded him wildly as he climbed down from the machine on to the beach. Harry spent some time checking over the machine generally and made some adjustments to the elevator controls. Undaunted and satisfied that all was in order, he made another ½ mile flight out and back along the strand to the further acclaim of the spectators and this ended his flying for the day. On each of the next two days he made flights of 1 mile, testing out the adjustments he was continually making to improve his machine's flight characteristics. Such was his keenness that the second of these two flights was made in semi-darkness. The next day was too stormy for any flying, but on Thursday 14th July, as the wind had abated, he was able to carry out a series of short flights and one widely sweeping flight at a height of 30 ft, which caused observers to comment positively on the improvement in the machine's flying capacity and in Harry's piloting skills. As will be seen Harry was in fact working up to meet a specific challenge.

Newcastle in County Down, where famously the mountains of Mourne sweep down to the sea, was a particularly well known holiday resort in 1910, and with the advent of the railway connection to Belfast it had also become a popular destination for

The Mark ID on arrival at Donard Park, Newcastle still has its transportation cradles in place. Note the tailfin, pointed elevator and covered front fuselage

day trippers. The Newcastle Council, anxious to develop the town's summer trade, had charged their Sports Committee with providing a range of activities and attractions to this end and the Committee was looking for a special attraction over and above the athletics, cycling and band competitions normally provided. Providentially, news reached them about Harry Ferguson's flying activities at Magilligan and the large crowds he was attracting there. They quickly made contact with him and after some brisk negotiations he agreed to exhibit his aeroplane at Newcastle over the three days, Thursday 21st, Friday 22nd and Saturday 23rd July, giving demonstration flights as conditions permitted. This was exactly what the Committee had been looking for, as flying exhibitions were very much the rage all over the UK and on the Continent, and almost no one in Ireland had even seen an aeroplane, let alone seen one in flight. The fact that Harry was a local and was very widely known for his successes in motoring competitions was an added bonus.

As a further incentive to both Harry and potential visitors, a prize of £100 was offered for a minimum 2 mile flight in a straight line, which would be billed as The First Official Aeroplane Flight in Ireland and the whole event was advertised by the Sports Committee as a Grand Aerial Display and Sports Meeting, and would take place just to the west of the town centre in Donard Park, part of the Earl of Annesley's demesne. It should be noted that £100 in 1910 would be worth in the region of £10,000 at today's values.

Harry in front of his Mark ID in Donard Park, Newcastle, newly arrived from Magilligan, c. 18th July 1910. Harry is recovering from a slight accident at Magilligan. The Clarke propeller is clearly shown

Harry's intense series of flights at Magilligan, finishing on 14th July, had been focused on his forthcoming commitment at Newcastle and on the attempt to win the £100 prize. On Friday 15th July he had the aeroplane dismantled and dispatched to Newcastle. It is not known precisely when the machine was delivered to the fenced-off part of Donard Park allocated to it, but re-assembly was commenced on Monday 18th. Harry made his base at the Slieve Donard Hotel close to the beach at the Newcastle end of Dundrum Bay, while his small team of assistants were accommodated near to Donard Park, it being likely that they shared night duty in the stores tent beside the aeroplane to ward off souvenir hunters.

It must be said that although the part of Donard Park nearest the town was at that time relatively open and level parkland, it was it by no means extensive in terms of flying and it certainly would not have permitted a two mile flight in any form within its confines, let alone in a straight line. The layout of athletics tracks and the expected presence of very large numbers of spectators would place further restrictions on the space available. Added to this was the proximity of 2800 ft high Slieve Donard mountain and its associated peaks, just one and a half miles to the south west, which were known to create unpredictable downdraughts and gusts from the prevailing south westerlies. Clearly not an ideal location for any flying endeavour, especially for a relatively inexperienced aviator in an underpowered aeroplane with only basic controls. Although Harry had a thrusting and rather reckless attitude at times, prepared to take chances, it would seem likely that he well knew that he could do little more than short demonstration hops in Donard Park and that he had his sights on the beach of Dundrum Bay for any real attempt on the £100 prize, and in the end this is how things worked out. The beach along Dundrum Bay stretches three miles in a north easterly direction from Newcastle to the mouth of Dundrum's inner bay and is rather similar to the Magilligan strand with its shallow gradient exposing around 200 yards of sand at low tide. It is similarly backed by sand hills. One advantage of the Dundrum beach is its south west orientation, the prevailing wind direction, but this is offset by the looming presence of Slieve Donard with its gusts and downdraughts as previously mentioned. See Appendix 9.

Although it seems from available information that Harry had undertaken to demonstrate his aeroplane on each of the three days, 21st, 22nd, and 23rd July, it was only on Saturday 23rd that he attempted to fly. This may have been on account of the weather conditions which were quite unsettled. Bearing in mind the limited flying capacity of his aeroplane, this three day arrangement may have been planned for just such a delay. Be that as it may, many people who were arriving in Newcastle each day in anticipation of seeing him fly were already feeling let down and by Saturday, when very large crowds were arriving on the excursion trains, an element of scepticism and disquiet was already in the air.

During Saturday afternoon the weather remained so severe that not even Harry dared to make any attempt to fly. As the hours passed by, the crowd, lacking any real understanding of the limits of an early aeroplane such as Harry's, grew increasingly restless and eventually overran the protective fence around the aeroplane, forcing a squad of the Royal Irish Constabulary to take charge of the volatile situation. After a while most of the disappointed onlookers gradually dispersed to watch some of the other events taking place in the Park and elsewhere in Newcastle. Meanwhile Harry and his assistants disconnected the wings from the fuselage and, under police escort, transported it to the seafront between the Slieve Donard Hotel and the beach proper, still retaining a motley entourage of the more curious and determined spectators. Re-assembly of the machine was started immediately and as soon as the wings were in place and the rigging and control wires fully checked it was manhandled down on to the beach itself. The strong wind still persisted, incurring more waiting for the watchers who were again getting restless, until Harry decided at 7.45 pm, against the advice of his colleagues, that he would make an attempt to fly and climbed into the cockpit. His helpers, well drilled in the starting procedures, manned the propeller, the wingtips and the rear fuselage. On a signal from Harry the propeller was swung and the engine broke into life with its unsilenced clattering roar. On a further signal, as soon as the engine had settled into a steady rhythm, the machine was allowed to start forward, with the helpers moving clear. Gaining speed rapidly the machine rose to 10 ft or so but after staggering in the gusts for about 50 yards it was driven down on to the sand, breaking the propeller and one of its mainwheels. Having replaced the damaged parts Harry taxied out once more, but on rising to a height of 12 ft he was again forced down, more heavily this time and at an angle, wrecking one of the wings. This time the damage was such that no further attempts could be made that day and the machine was taken off the beach for repair. Although the by now large crowd of watchers had experienced some excitement, it was not what they'd come for and they reluctantly left the scene expressing their feelings with a mixture of stoic disappointment and outright scepticism, sometimes clothed with ribald witticisms.

It was not in Harry's nature to accept this sort of situation lying down and with the crowds' displeasure ringing in his ears he started immediately the next day to repair the machine, using the Slieve Donard Hotel as a base. Within three days on 26th July he was ready to try again and the machine was taken down on to the

Harry with the Mark
I D on the beach at
Newcastle in July 1910,
after an early mishap
which damaged a
wheel and broke the
Clarke propeller

sands and made ready, although the conditions were still far from suitable. Following the usual drill it was released and after a run of 200 yards into the 20 mph wind he lifted it into the air and was able to fly for about half a mile at heights varying between 5 ft and 30 ft. However towards the end of the short flight the aeroplane was almost overturned by a very sharp gust and, although he managed to right it, the subsequent landing was rather heavy and he was left with two buckled wheels and a broken stay.

The deadline for the £100 prize was the end of July and time was running out. The Sports Committee were well aware of the crowd's displeasure at Harry's failure to perform, but they had also seen the extra influx of visitors that his presence had generated and to be fair, they had also recognised the strenuous efforts Harry had made and had seen his genuine frustration at not being able to demonstrate his aeroplane in a proper flight. After some consideration the Committee decided to extend the prize deadline until the end of August, and this gave Harry some breathing space.

There are no reports of Harry's continuous presence in Newcastle before he next attempted to fly there almost two weeks later, so it would seem likely that he took his machine back to the workshop in Belfast for a thorough overhaul. It had been literally in the field for almost four months and had undergone many repairs during that time, so such a checkup was not before time. At Newcastle alone he had incurred breakages that included two wings, three propellers, great lengths of rigging wire and the severe buckling of eight wheels. Always aware of his aeroplane's limited power he took this opportunity to look for ways to reduce its weight and he stated that before he went back to Newcastle he was able to make savings of around 50 lbs. Looking at the machine's basic structure and lack of frills it is not obvious how this might have been achieved. Perhaps he left off his long johns and some of his ego!

On Monday 8th August he was back on the strand at Newcastle really determined to show that he was a proper aviator and to win the £100 prize, although in truth, he must have spent almost as much as that amount in trying to win it. The conditions being fair he had the machine manhandled on its wheels right back along the beach to the Dundrum end, leaving a full three miles of beach over which, with good luck and good guidance, he could fly at least two miles and win the prize. Made ready as before and released, he took it up quickly to 40 ft and then further up to about 100 ft to get clear of downdraughts and flew well over two miles along the strand at 30 to 40 mph, landing safely on the sand just past the Slieve Donard Hotel at the Black Rock. The large crowd of holidaymakers and other spectators who had somehow managed to hear of the latest attempt and were lining every vantage point along the seafront and in the sand hills went mad with enthusiasm, mobbing the conquering hero and his machine. When he was able to dismount the enthusiastic crowd good humouredly chaired him back to his base at the hotel. Changed times!

Although Harry was fired up after his success at Newcastle and expressed his intention of returning to Magilligan as soon as possible to continue testing and improving the aeroplane and developing his piloting technique, he did not return there immediately. Instead he took it back to the Chichester Street workshop, as he planned some further modifications and these could be more easily carried out there. Like other aviators in those early days Harry had found that propellers were easily broken due to tipping up on landing. The engine weight, well forward as in most monoplanes, combined with poor landing surfaces and the use

Harry with the Liverpool actress, Rita Marr, in front of the Mark 1E in which she was given a flight at Magilligan on 23rd August 1910. Rita is posing in her stylish overcoat which displays its low slung modesty belt – a fashion created following Press photographs of notable ladies with their skirts suitably restrained before flights. Harry's white flying suit also has a certain style

of narrow-tyred bicycle type wheels which could bite in, were the basic causes of such noseovers. Antoinette and others had sought to prevent this action and to protect their propellers by providing a forward projecting hockey stick skid under the nose of their aircraft, and indeed on Harry's Mark 1, even though the main wheels were further forward than at present, a rudimentary hockey stick had been provided. He had removed it when he simplified the first, rather complicated main undercarriage, to Mark 1A standard and he now reinstated the hockey stick in a more effective form, projecting it well forward of the propeller arc and braced by a pair of V struts from the bottom longerons at the first fuselage frame. The unsprung tailwheel was omitted in favour of a tail skid which angled down at about thirty degrees to the bottom of the rudder post from the third fuselage frame in front of it and extended about 18 ins to the rear. Perhaps rather surprisingly he removed the fabric tailfin of the previous version. He reversed the positions of the pilot and the passenger, leaving the pilot seated between the pylons. With this overhauled and slightly modified version, illustrated on drawing No 5 and classified as Mark 1E, he returned to Magilligan around 22nd August and resumed his flying programme on 23rd, when he made a number of short flights. On one of these he carried a Liverpool actress, Rita Marr, as passenger, this being the first officially recorded passenger flight in Ireland. On Thursday 25th August having completed a one mile flight at a height of 30 ft he landed to make some adjustments. On attempting to restart the engine it ignited at a weakness in the petrol supply pipe and damage was caused to some engine accessories before the fire could be doused. Clearly a dangerous

moment which could have been fatal if it had happened in flight. This incident put a stop to further flying, as replacements for the damaged accessories had to be ordered from the manufacturer in England. However the delay that this caused was not overly frustrating as he was required to help out a special flying event on 29th and 30th August at Leopardstown near Dublin.

Harry flying the Mark 1E towards Magilligan Point over the Back Strand, late summer 1910. Note the new hockey stick front skid and pilot now seated between the pylons

An Interlude,
a Summer of Progress,
then … Disaster

On 5th November 1909 a number of Irishmen interested in aviation had got together and formed the Aero Club of Ireland. The prime mover and true founder was J. C. Percy, previously mentioned in this account. Other early members who formed the first committee with J. C. Percy were; John Dunville, Edward White, Walter Sexton, Major Wellesley and Harry Ferguson, with John Dunville being elected first chairman. John Dunville, scion of the wealthy Belfast whiskey distilling family, would in 1910 make a fine 5 hour crossing of the Irish sea in a hydrogen balloon, during which he reached an altitude of 10,000 ft. Dunville was already a committee member of the Royal Aero Club in London, providing a useful link between the two organisations.

Early in 1910 J. C. Percy conceived the idea of a first Irish Flying Meeting and convinced the Aero Club of its desirability and its potential for increasing air consciousness in Ireland. After dealing with the problems of competing with promoters in England

and Scotland for participating aviators, trying to find a venue in Ireland and above all finding finance, their hard work eventually paid off and it was established that a two-day Flying Meeting would take place at Leopardstown Racecourse just six miles outside Dublin, on Monday and Tuesday 29th and 30th August. The Leopardstown venue was far from ideal for the primitive aircraft of the day, being close to the Dublin and Wicklow mountains with their potential for creating downdraughts and rapid changes of wind direction, while the course itself was surrounded by mature trees on three sides and the remaining side contained grandstands with their fenced enclosures. The so-called aerodrome space within the course was bisected by a substantial hedge and there were further fences and two minor roads crossing it. Nevertheless it was the best on offer and at least it was convenient for spectators, due to its proximity to Dublin and the connecting railway station nearby.

Three well known aviators were contracted to appear; American Armstrong Drexel, Englishman Capt. Bertram Dickson and Cecil Grace of Irish parentage. Two Grace brothers, William Russell and Michael Paul, had emigrated to America from Ireland with their wives in 1850 and within a surprisingly few years had built up a prosperous shipping business on the west coast of North and South America. Their younger brother John William and his

Harry and James Valentine looking over Drexel's two-seat Bleriot in advance of the first Irish Flying Meeting at Leopardstown Racecourse on 29th and 30th August 1910. Unfortunately due to illness Drexel was unable to display his machine in flight wife joined them around 1875 and their son Cecil was born in Valparaiso in Chile in 1880. The Grace business developed into banking and insurance and the Grace Shipping Line became famous all over the world, with the family becoming extremely wealthy and influential in New York where they had their headquarters. On the death of his father in New York in 1904, Cecil and his mother returned to England, where he completed his education at Oxford before becoming fascinated by the new world of aviation. He bought and learnt to fly on one of the six Wright 'Flyers' built by the Short Brothers in their factory at Leysdown on the Isle of Sheppey in Kent in 1909-10. While in Ireland for the Leopardstown Meeting he stayed with his cousin Sir Valentine Grace at Monkstown, County Dublin.

Drexel arrived with two Bleriot monoplanes, a single seater and a two seater on which passenger flights would be given, while Dickson and Grace brought Farman biplanes, both also able to take passengers. Due to his aeroplane being out of action following the fire at Magilligan, Harry could not take part at Leopardstown as a pilot, but being a committee member he was much involved as an official steward. With the tremendous interest in this flying novelty and the lack of public understanding of the limitations and potential dangers associated with aeroplanes, tight marshalling and supervision of the crowds was essential, so stewarding was an important task. By mid morning on Monday the Course was thronging with spectators at every vantage point, paid and unpaid, although strenuous efforts had been made to defeat the latter! An amusing entrepreneurial episode occurred in the general enclosure at one point, when an ancient fruit seller, during a lull in her sales, heard men announcing "Official Programmes," and started calling out "Official Apples," to accelerate her sales.

Although the weather was far from kind all three pilots were able to demonstrate their aircraft before the great crowd at some time on the Monday, with limited passenger carrying flights being made by Grace. On the Tuesday it was very blustery but Grace managed to give what was generally agreed to be the display of the Meeting. The following eye-witness account by a *Flight* magazine reporter is included as it conveys a vivid yet accurate picture of this flight;

'…In an exceedingly strong and gusty wind Mr Grace rose on his
Farman biplane, head to wind, then fought his way over the finishing straight [in front of the grandstand] and well out towards the
mountains, making leeway and dropping into the trough then rising on the crest of the viewless air-waves, which also treacherously
attacked him sideways as though in wantonly mischievous mood,
causing the machine to roll like a ship in a heavy sea. When he had
gone so near the hills that it became needful to turn, he did not
come round head to wind but made to the leftward, so that presently he had the wind in his wake. Then the biplane seemed suddenly to shoot ahead for, with the following gusts, the rate of travel
of course became instantly at least thrice as fast as it had been
on the other tack. He continued this way for a mile or more at a
speed that must have been at least 60 miles an hour in relation to
the land below. Then he made a wide sweep, still over the trees,
and fought his way once more round the course, the constant activity of his hand at the flying control lever revealing how instant
and how forceful were the prankish forces of nature that were
being pitted against the prowess – one had well-nigh said imper-
tinence – of man. Just as he came over the heads of the onlookers, the biplane gave a great plunge into the trough of a gust, the
spectacle being remarkable, for as the biplane pitched, the loudly
cheering onlookers evidently thought it would be impossible to re-
cover her and their cheers stopped as though some invisible force
had instantly muffled each mouth as one. It is strange to behold a
vast concourse of people catch its breath as one person, that time
when their hearts leap with apprehension. Despite the enormous
strains that flying in this sort of weather must impose on a machine, the biplane with the clipped under mainplane answered to
the control of the pilot, who got her away from over the spectators
and began putting her up the finishing straight, when he encoun-
tered worse gusts on worse. But after passing in front of the Royal
box, Mr Grace was able, by a combination of great skill, fine nerve
and good luck, to land her without even touching the fencing'.

Later in the afternoon Capt. Dickson took to the air and, attempting to keep well within the view of the crowd, was crossing
the inner space at right angles when the aircraft was hit by a sharp

gust and he was forced to make an extremely steep descent, with the engine cut off, in order to get down safely between the fences. This dramatic descent, so expertly handled, greatly appealed to the crowd. Due to illness Drexel was unable to fly but his two Bleriots were put on static display. It is of interest to know that Capt. Dickson's fee was £500 (for circular flying!), while Drexel and Grace each got £250. These were considerable amounts and would equate to something like £40,000 and £20,000 in present day terms. The agreement to pay Dickson double for circular flying highlights the still primitive ability of pilots and machines to carry out manoeuvres easily in a restricted airspace. Dickson was the most experienced of the three aviators and clearly he was expected to perform in this way, while the others were to be allowed greater freedom of manoeuvre.

Harry must have been watching and learning from all these activities and from his close contact with the three experienced aviators. It is a measure of his position within the flying fraternity that he was invited to the dinner being given by the Corinthian Club in honour of the three visiting aviators on the Monday evening, at which the already well known J. T. C. Moore-Brabazon was also a guest. J. T. C. Moore-Brabazon, who was born in County Meath, was a leading aviator of the day, being the first holder of an official pilot's licence as issued by the Aero Club of England, later the Royal Aero Club. He had a long and distinguished life in aviation and was later honoured as Lord Brabazon of Tara for services rendered to that cause.

After the Leopardstown Flying Meeting Harry took a brief holiday before returning to Magilligan to prepare his aeroplane for a further programme of flying. The engine had to be set up again with the replacement accessories and the aircraft had to be re-rigged and generally checked over. By Sunday 11th September Harry was again ready to resume flying at Magilligan.

The contemporary account quoted in relation to Cecil Grace's flight at Leopardstown was from a report by a knowledgeable aeronautical correspondent. The reports of Harry's next flights at Magilligan are by one of the *Coleraine Chronicle's* general reporters describing a very new spectacle. One can be concerned that such reporters may lack understanding or get carried away by the excitement of it all, and accuracy may suffer! Fortunately in this instance this newspaper's reporter produces a very sensible and informative account of Harry's efforts in their issue of 11th September, which is in every way worth quoting;

'Many spectators witnessed a resumption on Sunday of Mr Ferguson's experiments in aviation at Magilligan Point, where he returned recently after officiating at the Aero Club's successful aviation meeting at Leopardstown after a brief holiday.

The weather was delightfully fine, but a twelve mile fluky wind from the north-east blew across the strand. About half past five o'clock Mr Ferguson started his engine and dashed along the beach. After making a number of short flights he steered his craft along the water's edge, and at once rose to about 25 ft, and flew steadily for a mile, part of his course lying over Lough Foyle. While in full flight he swung smartly to the left and executed a complete circle in mid-air, and made his way back to his starting point. As he neared the lofty sand-dunes on his homeward run the 'plane began to fall, and after a brief struggle with the invisible, the aviator was forced to alight and complete the run on the strand. Just as he reached his starting point a tyre burst, and as the hour was advanced, work was suspended for the day.

Adverting to his flights on Sunday, Mr Ferguson said that many people doubted the existence of 'air pockets' and down-currents in the atmosphere. "I myself, witnessed a striking proof of their presence", he said, "on Sunday, prior to the Leopardstown aviation meeting. On that day, on the famous course there, Drexel, using a machine 100lbs. lighter, and employing 20 hp more than mine, was unable to rise to any appreciable altitude, although he made repeated attempts. His failure was due to a down-current, such as I experienced today".

Mr Ferguson hopes to make short flights daily for the next fortnight, provided the atmospheric conditions are suitable'.

This gives a very good picture of Harry's flights and shows how he is getting more proficient in his aerial manoeuvres. It also gives a little insight into how aviators were getting to understand the currents of air, a new invisible medium that was just opening up. These early aviators were pioneers in every sense, risking their reputations and their lives opening up the new frontier of the air. A further quotation from the same reporter in the *Coleraine Chronicle's* issue on Saturday, 24th September 1910, is even more interesting and informative.

FERGUSON'S FLIGHTS

Belfast Airman's Exciting Experiences.

'Favoured by excellent atmospheric conditions, Mr Harry G. Ferguson, the Belfast aviator, performed a number of interesting flights on the beach at Magilligan Point (Co. Derry) every day last week, with the exception of Tuesday when the weather was unsuitable. On Monday and Wednesday afternoons a variety of mid-air manoeuvres were performed, such as right and left hand turns, circling at full speed, etc., the daily aggregate distance amounting to about ten miles, and the longest flight approximately two miles. Similar work was done on Thursday. On Friday afternoon a rather exciting experience befell Mr Ferguson. He had attained a height of 30 ft in a 20-mile wind when a heavy gust suddenly struck the monoplane, causing it to heel over in a most alarming manner, the horizontal wings being forced into an almost vertical position. It was an anxious moment for the spectators, who feared that a disaster was about to happen before their gaze. Mr Ferguson, however, who was handling the machine superbly, was equal to the occasion, righting his craft with a movement of his warping lever which, by increasing the aero-curve of the sinking wing, and correspondingly decreasing the aero-curve of the ascending wing, restores the lateral balance of the craft by wind resistance, and causes it to assume an even keel. Completing the flight in safety, the airman alighted, to the relief of the onlookers. On Wednesday, Thursday and Friday afternoons Mr Ferguson made short ascents with passengers, one being a lady. His work on Saturday, being accomplished in beautifully fine weather, was witnessed by many spectators, the longest flight being a mile. On Sunday the atmospheric conditions were not suitable.'

Pilot and Passenger in Thirty-mile Wind.

'Although a treacherous wind, varying in velocity from ten to thirty miles an hour, blew from the north-west on Wednesday, Mr Ferguson, the Belfast aviator, performed pretty flights at Magilligan Point during the forenoon and evening, the machine behaving excellently, despite the severe buffeting it received. The mono-plane, however, was subjected to a more severe trial when Mr Ferguson essayed ascents with a passenger. The present engine – a 35 hp eight-cylindered JAP – it may be stated, is not power-ful enough to carry passengers for long distances, but running along the ground with the tail of the machine raised in the air by means of the elevator, the angle of incidence of the wing is re-duced so that very high speeds can be attained with the less-ened wind resistance, and whilst travelling thus, if the elevating plane is raised the tail sinks, causing the machine to ascend and carry its double burden for a considerable distance in flight.

Mr Ferguson's invitation to accompany him was accepted by the writer, who found a precarious perch on the chassis of the ma-chine close behind the pilot. Then the engine was started, and with open throttle, the machine tore over the sloppy strand at fully forty miles an hour, the rapidly revolving wheels slinging up a moist mixture that liberally bespattered the low seated passenger. Then almost imperceptibly the ascent was made, the sensation of flight being delightfully exhilarating as the speed of the machine acceler-ated to 50 miles an hour as it ran before the wind, the back-wash of the propeller in its 1,600 revolutions a minute making aviation a very draughty means of locomotion. Swerving round in a semi-circle, a number of short flights were made in the teeth of the wind, practically vibration ceasing as the machine slid upwards into the element it strove to conquer. With the engine roaring might-ily, the little craft burrowed into the wind, its occupants being enveloped in the thin stream of blue-tinted odorous smoke and burnt gas that belched from the engine; while the wind pressure was excessive. It was very interesting to observe the work of the pilot, executed with deftness, and lightning rapidity, movements of the pedal-operated steering gear, the elevating-wheel, the warp-ing lever, and the air-port lever crowding each other, or happening simultaneously, the running of the engine being all the while under observation, and, in addition, watch kept unremittingly on the wind conditions, all making the work of the aviator no sinecure. After

Experimental Mark
1F with JAP engine in
raised position and
front fuselage formed
into an inverted
triangular cross section.
Magilligan summer 1910

about an hour's work with his passenger, Mr Ferguson, as sole occupant, manipulated his monoplane in a series of graceful flights,
which were repeated in the evening. He hopes to make a series of
flights on Sunday, without fail, as a set-off to the disappointment
of last Sunday, when the weather conditions precluded ascents.'

The atmosphere at Magilligan with its difficulties and its excite-
ments is clearly portrayed in this report, while the description of
the use and effect of the controls is very well covered when one
considers how little of this detail was known outside the aviators
themselves in 1910, and even they were learning the hard way.
It is noted that the passenger position is now behind the pilot as
the reporter clearly describes *perching perilously behind the pilot*.
He also describes it as being *a very draughty means of locomotion*
and being *enveloped in a thin stream of blue-tinted odorous smoke
and gas*, conjuring up a convincing, if slightly amusing and perhaps understated, picture of the actuality of early flying, whizzing along, completely exposed in an light wooden framework.
One marvels that he observed so much! He confirms that the elevator is still operated by a hand wheel, but that the wing warping control is now worked by a lever.

Also shown is Harry's complete absorption in flying at that time,
with his aeroplane out every day that weather permitted. Although
it is certain that Harry enjoyed the excitement and challenge that
flying offered, there seems little doubt that he considered that

aviation had a future and that he had a part to play in it, and he continued trying to improve his aeroplane as his flight experience grew. Almost every day there would have been adjustments and repairs to be made to the machine and all this work had to be done with the limited facilities available in this exposed location in autumn conditions. The dedication and commitment of Harry and his assistants is indeed convincing.

At some time during this period at Magilligan Harry tried out a relocation of the JAP engine, raising it approximately nine inches to set its thrust line just below the upper longeron level, with the petrol tank being raised in unison so that it was within the fuselage. In con-

Harry, in the now familiar white flying suit, relaxes at the nose of his Mark 1E

junction with this move the engine bay framework was tapered into a narrow inverted triangular section at the front of the engine. Where before only the tops of the cylinders and the characteristic JAP fuel distribution pipework projected above the upper longerons, now the cylinders were entirely exposed. Overheating was a known problem with these engines, causing a loss of power all to quickly. It would seem that Harry was attempting to ameliorate this problem by exposing the cylinders to more of the cooling airflow. Bearing in mind that the exhaust gasses were emitted directly out of the cylinder heads, which were now directly in line with the pilot's face, it is perhaps not surprising that this modification was quickly abandoned. Although this version seems to have been short-lived, its triangular nose section will be seen in a later Ferguson aeroplane, and it is therefore illustrated as Mark 1F on drawing No 6.

Harry carried out all his remaining flights at Magilligan throughout September and into October in the Mark 1E machine. Again we can do no better than to quote from a *Coleraine Chronicle* report from their issue of 15th October 1910 to get a picture of the most significant events there during this period.

Harry flying in Mark IE towards Bellarena over the tidal sands at Magilligan, late summer 1910. The pilot's poisition, now located between the upper pylons, can be clearly seen

MID-AIR MANOEUVRES AT MAGILLIGAN

Ferguson's Fine Flights with Passenger

English Expert's Tribute

'Mr Harry G. Ferguson, the Belfast aviator, gave a meritorious exhibition of airmanship on the huge strand at Magilligan Point on Sunday afternoon, in the presence of a large assemblage of spectators, his work on that day marking in some respects a distinct advance on anything he has yet accomplished, especially as regards passenger-carrying; while he made one of the best flights he has yet done, solus, gaining the plaudits of the interested onlookers.

Mr T. W. K. Clarke, A.M.I.C.E. (Kingston-upon-Thames), the well-known aeronautical engineer and designer, principal of the Clarke aeroplane factory, and manufacturer of the famous propeller bearing his name, was present, being on a week-end visit to Mr Ferguson, and made his first flight as a passenger with the Belfast airman, the trip being the best yet accomplished under the double burden. The monoplane with Mr Ferguson as pilot, and Mr Clarke as passenger, rose to a height of 25 or 30 ft and flew steadily for about a mile, when it alighted, and after turning round, again rose, attaining the same height, soared back to the starting-point. After alighting Mr Clarke expressed his pleasure at making his first ascent under the auspices of Ireland's plucky and persevering young airman. "I had a nice trip," he said; "it was the best flying I have seen performed with an engine of less than 50 hp. Mr Ferguson is the only aviator I know who has himself designed, built and flown an aeroplane. He certainly deserves to succeed". With a new propeller in use, a similar trip was made, after which Mr Ferguson, as sole occupant, made a pretty flight, rising to a height of 50 ft, flew at that altitude for a mile, then made a splendid turning in mid-air, and returned to his starting-place. He complained of experiencing some trouble by the 16-mile wind interfering with his fore-and-aft stability. Starting off again, Mr Ferguson flew alongside the high sand-dunes, towards which he rapidly drifted, so close, indeed, that the spectators thought he would be dashed against them. However, he rose above them in time, and flew for about a mile at a height of 40 ft, then turned to the right and soared over the waters of Lough Foyle for a quarter of a mile, made a beautiful turning, heading towards the spectators lining the dunes, turned towards the left again, swung along the tide, and landed after cleverly completing a figure-of-eight manoeuvre in mid-air, the total distance of flight being three miles. It was one of the best – certainly the prettiest – flights by the Belfast man. Darkness now caused a cessation of work.'

ALARMING AEROPLANE ACCIDENT

Mr Harry G. Ferguson Injured

Disaster Follows Finest Exploit

'Disaster ever dogging the doings of the aviators, has overtaken the Belfast airman, just as he had achieved his greatest triumph in his plucky attempts to conquer the air. While his originally-designed Belfast-built monoplane is wrecked, we are glad to find he has escaped a fate only too frequently recorded of late in aerial chronicles. As it is he has sustained very considerable injuries, and is under medical treatment.

It appears that at Magilligan on Monday afternoon when Mr Clarke A.M.I.C.E. the well-known engineer, was about to leave for England no car was available, and Mr Ferguson pluckily and resourcefully undertook to carry Mr Clarke as passenger on his monoplane to Bellarena to catch the train – the first time a passenger ever travelled by aeroplane to catch a train. Accordingly Mr Ferguson took his passenger on board and set off along the strand to Bellarena, a distance of five miles. The 'plane behaved splendidly, flying beautifully at 40 ft, and the distance had almost been completed when the petrol supply proved faulty, occasioning a descent. It was found that the ground on which the machine had alighted was too rough to permit of a re-ascending with passenger. Mr Ferguson having practically accomplished his purpose, decided to fly back the five miles to his headquarters at Magilligan Point, and again started his 35 hp engine and, quickly rising from the ground, soared steadily homewards at a height of 80 ft Mounting higher and higher he attained an altitude of 200 ft his greatest height, and completed his record trip with a superb vol-plane, diving down and alighting exactly in the wheel tracks of the road on which the machine is hauled daily from the beach. After allowing his engine a few minutes to cool, Mr Ferguson set out on what proved his fateful flight, intending to execute circling manoeuvres in mid-air. He had only got about a half-mile on his way, at a height of 30 ft, when a gust of wind struck his machine squarely on the front, and as he was at the time lifting the 'plane higher by the elevator, the gust caused the craft to rise up sharply in the air, and assume an almost perpendicular position, truly a trying moment for the aviator. The result of the machine's vertical position as the speed fell off, and it swayed over on the left wing and came down sideways. Mr Ferguson's coolness did not desert him. Keeping the engine at full speed, and doing everything necessary to retrieve the situation, he would have succeeded had the monoplane been higher in the air, for he had caused the machine to assume a horizontal position, and was gathering up speed when the machine crashed to the strand, alighting in the tide with terrific force. Mr Ferguson was flung violently from his seat, his face striking the left mast of the craft. From this he rebounded, and was pitched out of the chassis on to one of the shattered wings. Here he lay unconscious for some minutes, and when he had regained his senses he struggled to his feet, and made his way to the hotel, although suffering acutely, streaming with blood. It was at once seen that his condition was bad, and accordingly medical aid was telegraphed for, and Dr. Newell, of Moville, arrived in a short time, crossing Lough Foyle in a motor-boat from Greencastle. He found that Mr Ferguson had sustained concussion of the brain, a split lip, extensive bruises on the face, body and legs, his thighs being cut in addition, and ten-

dons of the legs bruised. The doctor ordered the patient to be
kept quiet in bed for a few days, and is in daily attendance on him.

The monoplane presented a sorry spectacle as it lay on the beach,
one shattered wing crumpled below it, and the other pointing
skywards perpendicularly, the body of the machine lying sideways.
The engine and landing wheels escaped injury despite the force of
the fall, a circumstance due to the immense strength of the design
embodied in the machine. The rere part of the chassis is splin-
tered into fragments and twisted askew, all the control wires being snapped; while the various wire stays of the ill-fated craft are
twisted and tangled, remarkably few of them being snapped. The
propeller, of course, is smashed, both blades being broken off at
the boss. The landing skid has also been involved in the wreckage. The fabric covering of the wings is torn and tattered, and one
bears abundant evidence of Mr Ferguson's injuries in the form of
blood stains. The machine will require extensive repairs, amounting practically to a re-building, before further flights can be made.

Interviewed on the following day in bed, Mr Ferguson, although
bandaged and sore, appeared to have regained his usual good
spirits, making light of his personal injuries, and referring re-
gretfully to the loss of his 'plane. Speaking of his sensations on
regaining consciousness, he said he at first had the impression that it was all a dream, and he was congratulating himself
that it was such, as he was fearing that his financial resources
would be unequal to making right his loss. Then with the recovery of his senses he found that it was no dream, but stern real-
ity. He has not considered yet what his future plans will be. He
attributes the disaster to the insufficiency of the power of the
engine, and states that if he had had a 50 hp engine, or had been
about 15 or 20 ft higher in the air, all would have been well.

There are surely many people in the North of Ireland, indeed in all of Ireland, interested in the doings of Mr Ferguson,
the only Irish aviator, who would be glad to learn of the initia-
tion of some fund for furthering and fostering his intrepid work.
The present time suggests itself as an opportune moment.'

Again the reporter's account is thoughtful, informed and graphic.

It is interesting to hear that Mr Clarke, who had already designed and built gliders for customers and was well known amongst all the prominent English aviators, had not yet ever flown. With the descriptions of Harry's circling and his figures-of-eight, it is clear that he is now flying quite freely when the conditions are in his favour, despite the limited power available to him. The reporter's account of the accident is particularly graphic and his description of how the monoplane's wing dropped away as airspeed was lost, is an accurate depiction of the classic stall, a problem manoeuvre not then fully recognised by aviators. Bearing in mind the suddenness and severity of the stall and the resultant crash, the statement that it was *'truly a trying moment for the aviator'* seems a bit of an understatement! In consideration of the 1910 date it is interesting to hear of the use of telegraphy to call medical assistance and the resultant prompt arrival of the doctor by boat. It would be many years before similar emergency assistance might be considered to have been improved. Harry's enthusiasm for the solution to Mr Clarke's transport problem can almost be sensed; the challenge, the demonstration of the practical use of his aeroplane and the chance to impress – and it worked. Nevertheless, let's visualize Mr Clarke whizzing through the air in his best business suit, perched precariously in the open fuselage with one hand for himself and one hand for his weekend Gladstone! After landing, when the engine had given up due to fuel feed problems – fortunately not far from the planned drop-off point – he presumably had to help to turn the plane around and, as soon as the petrol flow problem had been solved, swing the propeller and then steady the machine as Harry moved off, before walking the one and a half miles over unknown fields and along country lanes to the railway station. A different time and a different breed indeed.

Second Wind

The mention at the end of the *Coleraine Chronicle* report of Harry's nightmare worry about his financial resources and the cost of repair of his smashed machine is extremely appropriate at this stage in his career. Earlier in this account the question of whether Joe Ferguson had known of Harry's aeronautical ideas before he went to the USA in the autumn of 1909 was discussed. It does seem as if Harry started out on his first aeroplane in Joe's absence, but whatever the truth, Harry could not have carried on with his flying enterprises throughout 1910 without Joe's sanction, as although there were seven directors on the J. B. Ferguson Ltd. Board, of which Harry was still one, obviously as the Senior and Managing Director Joe would have had the final say. When Harry started out on this enterprise in late 1909 he was clearly convinced that there was a business future for J. B. Ferguson Ltd. in this new form of transport, but whether he fully foresaw the difficulties and the potential costs of the enterprise is a question. It would seem likely that with his confident and thrusting personality he would have felt that he could sweep through any difficulties and succeed relatively quickly, and that he tacitly set aside any consideration of the financial implications. However during 1910 his aeronautics have been a fairly constant drain on the business's finances and on the works facilities in Chichester street, while he himself had only occasionally been contributing to the motoring side of the business. He had resigned from his position of Works Manager in early 1910 to concentrate on his flying and it would therefore seem that his personal income derived only from his position as a Director, albeit a junior one, so it is certain that his financial position was not strong. During the year the stretched business relations between the two brothers, fuelled by intermittent personality clashes arising from their rather similar, strong characters, aggravated by their religious differences and an ongoing romantic rivalry, seems to be nearing crisis point. So the serious crash which smashed his aeroplane beyond repair must clearly have brought things to a head. Harry, always his own man, began to think about starting up his own motor business. He was confident that his reputation in motoring remained strong and had not been harmed in any way by his flying adventures. Fortunately his wealthy friend from early motoring days, T. McGregor Greer, was willing to back him financially and along with further smaller investments from John Williams and others, he was able to start trading as May Street Motors in early 1911, at 87 May street. (these vacant premises, previously a bakery owned by Messrs Wilson & Strain, were demolished in the late 1930s to make way for Telephone House). On Joe's insistence, backed by the J. B. Ferguson Ltd. Company laws, he was not permitted to use the family name, however within a year, bold as ever, he had changed the name to Harry Ferguson Motors Ltd.

Just the cars for Ireland:

STAR CARS

1911 Models:
10 h. p. 2-cylinder, 12, 12, 20, 25 h. p. 4-cylinder, £240 to £700.

Any Type of Body supplied.   Star Detachable Wood and Wire Wheels a speciality.

Write for Catalogue "D," post free
The STAR ENGINEERING CO., Ltd., Wolverhampton.

London Depot
The Star Motor
Agency, Ltd.,
24, 25, 26 Long
Acre, W. C.

Sole selling
rights for
the District
granted to
Autocars Ltd.,
102 Grafton St.

Belfast The
May Street
Motor Co., May
Street

Limerick
Glentworth
Garage, Lower
Glentworth St.

THE STAR TORPEDO

12 h.p. - £325.   15 h.p. - £360
Hood, Screen and Lamps extra

When Harry set up on his own in May Street, Belfast in 1911, Star Cars was his first agency and the first car he sold was a Star

Harry needed initially to concentrate on getting his business up and running but this seemed to happen very quickly, as agencies for Star and Darracq cars were soon obtained and it is on record that he sold his first car, a Star, from the May Street premises on 16th March 1911. Nevertheless, despite this business pressure and the loss of his first aeroplane, it is quite clear that his commitment to aviation was as strong as ever, a fact confirmed in his April 1911 Census Return* where he records his occupation as Aviator, and by June he had completed an entirely new aeroplane, just as he had promised a few days after his disastrous crash the previous October. It is not certain whether Harry started the construction of this new aeroplane while still at Chichester Street, but it seems very likely that he did, and that its commencement there was a factor in the business split-up. It is however certain that it was completed in May Street.

*The Census entry for 14 Hartington Street (quite close to Harry's May Street premises), where both Harry and John Williams were boarders, records Harry's religious profession as 'Materialist' and that of John Williams as 'Agnostic', while John's occupation is given as Motor Engineer (Master).

His second, Mark 2, aeroplane was very considerably a different aircraft to the Mark 1. It is possible to give a description of it from general arrangement drawings and data published in contemporary aeronautical magazines and from a number of surviving photographs, but fortunately this basic information can be expanded to a very great degree following detailed study of the non-flying replica on display at the Ulster Folk and Transport Museum at Cultra in Co. Down. This replica was constructed in 1972 by Capt. J. C. Kelly Rogers, the internationally famous trans-Atlantic commercial pilot following his retirement. It is considered to be an extremely accurate replica due to the detailed studies Kelly Rogers made before and during construction, and in particular due to the great assistance he received from Joe Martin who had helped Harry to build and fly the original aeroplane and was then living in retirement at 87 years of age in his home town of Dromore in Co. Down, less than 5 miles from Harry's birthplace at Growell and his first triumph at Hillsborough. Joe Martin was Harry's longest serving working assistant and had helped with the construction and flying of both of Harry's aeroplanes in all their forms. He was a talented practical engineer and was well placed to advise Kelly Rogers on all aspects of the replica's construction.

The Mark 2, again a monoplane, had a slender, 21'6" long, tapering fuselage of inverted triangular section carrying slightly tapered two-spar wings of 6'0" average chord, spanning 32'0". The wings had 21 ribs each side, shaped to the symmetrical Eiffel 31 aerofoil section and were supported from a single A frame cabane pylon, located centrally to the wing chord, 5'6" back from the nose. The substantial side members of the A frame extended 2'6" below the level of the bottom longeron to carry the main undercarriage wheels. Tubular metal frames from the main axle and from the bottom longeron projected forward to form a set of forks for the nosewheel, centrally positioned under the engine.

Although the three wheels were of equal diameter they did not form a true tricycle landing gear, as the aeroplane sat down on its tail skid when at rest, however as the nosewheel was little more than an inch or so above the mainwheels it is likely that all three wheels would have touched down to-

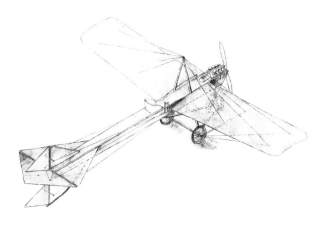

Isometric line drawing showing general layout of the Ferguson Mark 2

gether on landing. Certainly the nosewheel served to protect the propeller during any tendency to noseover, much as the projecting hockey stick skids on the earlier Marks.

The triangular tailplane and elevator were very similar to those on the Mark 1E, but the split upper and lower rudders were sharply pointed horizontal isosceles triangles instead of the trapezoidally-shaped ones used previously. A light strut sloped up from the top of the fuselage near the tail bracing the top of the rudder post, although the triangular space thus formed was not infilled to form a tailfin. A similarly angled strut beneath the tail braced the bottom end of the rudder post and finished as a curved tailskid. The pilot's seat with its curved backrest was positioned just to the rear of the wing trailing edge and was set high up due to the restricted space offered by the fuselage's triangular section. As this placed the pilot in a very exposed position, a restraining harness was provided, fixed to the fuselage decking behind the pilot's seat. A cramped passenger seat with footrest was located under the cabane pylon. The sides of the nose section of the fuselage below the engine were panelled with sheet metal to shield against the heat from the exhaust pipes with which the engine was fitted for the first time, projecting downwards from the cylinder heads, while the remainder of the fuselage sides and the decking from the cockpit to the tail were fabric covered. The overall appearance of Harry's Mark 2 aeroplane was closer to the Antoinette than to the Bleriot, but nevertheless was very much a Ferguson aircraft. It had the general outward appearance of being a more practical flying machine than the Mark 1 in any of its forms. The Ferguson Mark 2 is illustrated on drawing No 6.

The control of the rudders was now by a conventional rudder bar and the elevator was operated by a lever at the pilot's right hand, pivoted externally on the right upper longeron. For lateral control the tips of the mainplanes were warped from a laterally pivoting external lever at the pilot's left hand. This lever curved down vertically from the pilot's position and was connected to a tubular axle running forward under, and suspended from, the bottom longeron as far as the cabane pylon where it terminated in a pivoting lever. Cables from each end of this lever descended to the hollow mainwheel axle and were directed by small pulleys through the axle and out of the two wheel hubs to each rear spar near the wingtips. The warping force from these cables only exerted a downward pull on the rear spars when the lever was operated, the upward movement at the opposite tip being achieved through a continuous over-wing cable which passed through a pulley at the top of the cabane pylon linking both rear spars near each wingtip. As one tip was pulled down the opposite tip was raised by this continuous cable linkage. To accommodate this warping action the front spars from each wing were bolted firmly at a 4 degree dihedral angle into a hollow metal connecting member bracketed up rigidly from the upper longerons, while the similar connecting member carrying the rear spars was pivoted from a subsidiary metal bearer spanning between the two upper longerons (see Appendix 10). This allowed the trailing portions of the wings to flex and to vary the incidence on each wing equally and oppositely. Study of the relatively substantial wing structure and the rather torturous cabling systems on the replica raises concerns as to the amount of force that would have been required to warp the wings and the amount of flex that would have been achieved. Bearing in mind the low wing loading of the aircraft, positive lateral control would seem to have been essential. Kelly Rogers seems to have shared these concerns and describes how he tested the system when the replica was complete;

'When I first operated the warping lever I waited for the awful sound of cracking ribs and breaking spars, but need not have worried – everything worked as it should'.

Harry had found from experience with his first aeroplane that the nominal 35 hp of his JAP engine at 1200 rpm was barely sufficient power for consistent flight and how after quite a short running time even this amount of power was not being achieved. While his second aeroplane was being built he put his mechanical talent to work on improving the engine's performance. In an article by him on the JAP Engine published in *The Aeroplane* on January 14th 1912, he sets out in detail the problems with this engine and how he overcame them. This article with its more developed writing style is interesting not only for its insights into Harry's technical ability, but it also indicates an increasingly confident nature. This article is included in full for detailed study in Appendix 11, here it is sufficient to give a brief summary of the problems faced and how he tackled them.

In Harry's own words the problems were;

'Firstly, overheating after about seven minutes' running. Secondly, the flow of oil into the pilot's face, making flight almost impossible. Thirdly, the low horse-power developed by the engine after it has been running a few minutes, consequent on over-heating. Fourthly, the danger of fire: and Fifthly, the fact that the engine will not turn slowly.

When flying with my machine at Magilligan last year I always found that after five to seven minutes' flight the pistons would run perfectly dry, and this would be the case no matter how much oil I started off with in my crank case or how much I let run into the cylinders by the usual JAP Methods.'

The solutions to these problems, again using Harry's own words, were;

'Summed up, then, I got over my first trouble of over-heating by making the lubrication right. I got over the second trouble of oil flowing into the pilot's face by closing up the auxiliary ports and fitting exhaust pipes. I got over the third trouble of low horse-power by making the lubrication right and getting a more uniform mixture by closing the auxiliary exhaust ports and fitting a new carburettor. I got over my fourth trou-

ble of the danger of fire by closing the ports and fitting the carburettor below the engine; and, fifthly, as there are no auxiliary
ports, the engine will turn round at something below 200 rpm.'

When all these modifications were completed Harry carried out
some pulling tests with his favoured Clarke propeller, using the
higher 1600 rpm he had found to be the best working speed for
the modified engine. He estimated an improvement of approximately 20% in power output, giving the engine a rating of about
40hp.

Satisfied that he now had the engine running efficiently he had
it mounted at the nose of the new aircraft, fixed into two metal
cradles spanning between the top longerons. These semi-circular
cradles matched the soffit shape of the engine's crank case and
placed the thrust line of the engine level with the longerons' top
surfaces, lifting the cylinders fully clear of the fuselage to give
maximum cooling. The newly fitted exhaust pipes terminated
12" below the top longeron level, clear of the fuselage and discharging the exhaust gasses below the wings and away from the
pilot. The 8" diameter cylindrical petrol tank spanned across the
top longerons, 12" to the rear of the engine.

Fitted with its 7 ft diameter Clarke propeller his Mark 2 aeroplane was ready for a new season's flying.

When Harry gave his commitment to building a new and improved aeroplane shortly after his accident in October, he had expressed his intention of returning with it to Magilligan. However,
he had since realised the potential offered by the considerable expanse of tidal sands available at the head of Strangford Lough
at Newtownards just 10 miles from his works in Belfast, and he
was considering the establishment of a base there rather than at
Magilligan which, after all, was 60 miles away. On hearing of
this possibility the Committee of the North Down Agricultural
Society, sitting in Newtownards on Friday 19th May, discussed
the option of obtaining his agreement to appear at their Annual
Agricultural Show on Thursday 15th June. A brief account of this
meeting is recorded in the 26th May issue of the *Newtownards
Spectator;*

'The Chairman said the next item on the agenda was to consider the advisability of engaging an aviator for the show.

Mr Henry – Is anybody available ?

The Secretary, Mr Russell, said he had spoken to Mr Ferguson and asked him if he would be available to fly at the show. Mr Ferguson said he would, and after a good deal of conversation about terms, he said he would have his machine on the grounds at nine o'clock, and if the weather was too stormy so he could not fly, he would leave the aeroplane on exhibition during the day, the Agricultural Society paying him a small sum for same, and if he made a successful flight he would get a correspondingly larger sum.

Joe Martin posing proudly with the new Mark 2 at Newtownards in October 1911

Mr Milling – What would be the cost of engaging a successful aviator?

The Secretary – Well a successful aviator took £300 from Bangor for a few hops. Continuing, Mr Russell said there was a possibility of the Belfast and Co. Down Railway contributing something to the cost of engaging Mr Ferguson.

Mr Milling – Would we be liable if he would hurt anybody?

A member – There are a lot of people who would come to the show if they thought he would meet with a bad accident. [Nothing ever changes!].

On the motion of Mr Simms, it was resolved that the secretary make arrangements with Mr Ferguson to fly at the annual show'.

North Down Agricultural Society.

———

EIGHTH

ANNUAL SHOW,

AT NEWTOWNARDS,

THURSDAY, 15 JUNE.

———

In addition to the usual attractions, if the weather be favourable.

Mr. HARRY G. FERGUSON,

the Irish Aviator, will attempt a flight in his new Aeroplane, from the Show Grounds.

Newspaper announcement of the annual show of the North Down Agricultural Society in June 1911, at which flights by Harry were to be a main attraction. Unfortunately Harry's disastrous landing accident on the eve of the show meant that only the aeroplane's wreckage could be on display

A further incentive to Harry at this time was the offer from the Aero Club of Ireland of a £100 prize for the longest flight in excess of 25 miles achieved in Ireland before October 1911. If he was successful at the Newtownards Show some of his Mark 2 development costs would be covered and he felt confident that the Aero Club prize could also be won before October, – so onwards to Newtownards.

The Newtownards location, essentially today's aerodrome, was then, as now, roughly triangular in shape, with the town itself at its northern apex. The roads to Comber and Portaferry, radiating at 45 degrees from Newtownards south and south-east respectively, form two sides of the area while the third side is bounded by the northern foreshore of Strangford Lough. Prior to 1800 a good portion of this low lying area was poorly drained and liable to flooding from high tides, rendering much of it unsuitable for effective agricultural use. In the early 1800s Lord Londonderry, the head landlord, authorised the construction of a defensive sea barrier along the foreshore boundary, incorporating floodgates at the eastern end to accommodate water discharging from a drainage canal that had been provided to carry storm water away from the town itself, while at intervals towards its Comber road end there were non-return valves at outlets from some sub soil drainage that had been provided. This work was completed in 1811 and so by 1911 the land was being well used. It had been divided up into over one hundred fields ranging mainly from 2 to 5 acres in size, although there were 3 or 4 of about 13 acres. All were defined by low banks and rough hedges. In 1891 a group of local businessmen formed the Ards Recreational Society and got permission to develop a 20 acre site towards the north-western corner of the area. Their site was approximately 300 x 200 yards overall and ran parallel to the Comber road, although inset from it by about 100 yards. This ambitious facility included horse racing and trotting tracks and pitches for lacrosse, soccer, cricket and lawn tennis. Although potentially one of the largest open spaces on the area, it was divided up by some light fences defining the pitches and racing tracks, and its boundary was defined by a 7 ft high fence, along parts of which were sheds for animals, changing rooms for sportsmen, and on the side adjacent to the Comber road there was a small grandstand. It was in these Recreation Grounds that the North Down Agricultural society would be holding their Annual Show.

With the above exception, most of the other fields were let individually or in small groups to townsfolk and local farmers, but in 1911 one large farm occupied a major portion of the eastern half of the triangular area, south of what was later to become Castlereagh Park football ground. Mr James Miskelly, who farmed this land, lived in a substantial house with outbuildings to the south of his farm, close to the tidal barrier. The farm was accessed from the Portaferry road via a long lane starting at the later Castlereagh Park location. As the overall triangular area of land was, in the main, so broken up by small fields it would seem certain that Harry intended to use the tidal shore for his next flight trials much as he had done at Magilligan, and it is known that he arranged to use Mr Miskelly's farm as a convenient base near the shore where his machine could be taken for repairs and storage during his Newtownards trials. Contemporary reports say that he had a small hangar there, a simple wooden shed of sufficient size to hold the fuselage with the wings dismounted and to give protection when they were being worked upon. In recent times the original sea barrier has been heightened and armoured with large rocks, making direct access down on to the beach somewhat awkward, but originally it was just a grassed bank sloping gently down on to the sand over a narrow margin of stones and shingle. The established land behind the barrier was only marginally above the highest tide level, and the top of the barrier, along which there was a rough path, was little more than 2 ft above that. There was also a small access path from the farmyard on to the beach, so as can be seen on the map of the area, Harry would have had little difficulty in moving his machine to and from the shore.

In response to the Agricultural Society's request for a flying display Harry inspected the Recreation Ground where the show was

to take place. The nominal clear area within the horse racing tracks was approximately 260 x 160 yards, and although there were some fences defining play pitches within this area, these would not be needed during the Show and could be removed to give maximum clearance. After discussions with the Show organisers to clarify his needs he was able to confirm that, with the right weather conditions, he would have just sufficient space to make take-offs and landings. Bearing in mind he was going to be flying an untried machine in the presence of a large crowd of spectators and numerous competitors with their animals, it was quite a challenge.

Harry arrived at Newtownards with his Mark 2 aeroplane on Monday 12th June, accompanied by his friend and colleague John Williams. Joe Martin and another of Harry's mechanics, Sam Turkington, about whom little is known, travelled with them to help prepare the machine for flight. As soon as the tide started to recede the fuselage and wings were carried separately down on to the sand and work began to rig the wings and to connect and adjust the warping cables. Shortly after 6 pm it was ready and, despite a strong and gusting northerly wind, Harry was so keen to try out his new machine that he insisted on making a trial run right away. In the circumstances it is probable that Harry's intention was just to get the feel of the new aeroplane and its up-rated engine, in order to make any necessary adjustments before starting serious flight trials when conditions were

more suitable, for he took John Williams with him in the passenger's seat when he started off downwind in a southerly direction towards Island Hill, about two miles distant, and it seems unlikely that he would have burdened the untried machine with the additional load of a passenger on a first trial flight. The machine quickly gathered speed, running along the sand and splashing through the occasional puddle left by the tide until they were about a mile distant, when the machine was stopped and John Williams was seen to dismount. It was then turned into the wind and Harry started on the return run without Williams. A considerable crowd had gathered along the sea barrier and on the beach itself to savour the activities, but given the blustery conditions were not really expecting to see a flight. However almost immediately after the machine started to move it was lifted into the air by the combination of its low wing loading and the strong headwind, and very quickly it reached a height of about 50 ft. Battling to control his aeroplane as it was buffeted about, he made several attempts to make a safe landing but a combination of the machine's volatility in the wind and the random location of spectators along the beach made this difficult. As he neared the end of the beach he saw an opportunity and put the machine down quickly from about 20 ft damaging the undercarriage, some rigging and breaking the propeller. Fortunately Harry himself was not hurt. The machine was manhandled to his base at Miskelly's farm, and with the commitment to appear at the Agricultural Show in three day's time, work was started on repairs immediately.

On his return to Newtownards with his rebuilt Mark 2 in October 1911, Harry gave a number of passenger flights. On this occasion his passenger is Mrs Greer, wife of his friend and financial backer, T. McGregor Greer

By Tuesday evening these were complete and a new propeller had been fitted, and Harry had it taken down on to the beach for further trials. After several successful flights, on one of which he carried a passenger weighing 182 lbs (83 kg), he was satisfied that it was correctly set up and performing well, but he still needed to try it out in the more restricted confines of the Recreation Grounds. On Wednesday, in preparation for the following day's Show, he had his machine transported to the Showground and prepared for flight. In the evening as the wind eased he carried out a number of brief flights. At first he did some short runs within the grounds, and then, having got the feel of the space, he took off over the 7 ft high boundary fence, lifting off at the earliest moment, and landing back again after a brief circuit. Following a number of successful flights, on two occasions with passengers, he felt satisfied that he was now fully prepared for his demonstration on the next day, and decided to return for the night to his rudimentary base at Miskelly's farm by flying back to the beach. With Joe Martin in the passenger seat he took off on what seems to have been Joe's first flight, and flew back towards the shore rising to less than 25 ft for the short flight. Contemporary reports say that Harry attempted to land on a grassed area near the beach, and it is known that there was an piece of uncultivated ground which could be covered by the spring tides directly in line between the Recreation Grounds and the beach close to Miskelly's farm. The chosen surface proved to be softer than expected, the grass being boggy, and although the machine touched down safely, the wheels sank suddenly while the machine was still travelling at about 30 mph, tipping the machine up on its nose with considerable force and breaking many of the bracing wires, with the result that the wings and most of the fuselage were very badly damaged. Harry was saved from injury by the new harness at the pilot's seat, but the unfortunate

Joe Martin was knocked unconscious when he was thrown forward against the substantial cabane members, sustaining concussion, broken teeth, cuts to the head and much bruising. He was rushed to a local doctor who patched him up, but it was clear that he would not be fully recovered for a week or more, although he reassured an anxious Harry that he would be prepared to go up again as soon as he was fit.

The same could not be said about the aeroplane. Such was the extent of the damage it was clear that it could not be repaired in time for the next day's show. It was decided however, to transport the wreckage to the Showgrounds and to put it on display before the attending crowds, as a gesture of Harry's intent and endeavour. For most visitors it would have been their first sight of an aeroplane and without doubt a confusing one. Perhaps not a sight to encourage participation in the new flying enterprise! Nevertheless the association of Harry Ferguson's name with daring deeds and progressive thinking would have been further advanced in the public's mind, bolstered by his making it known that he intended to rebuild his machine and to return to Newtownards for more flight trials before the year was out. And he kept his promise, arriving back at Newtownards on Tuesday 17th October with the completely rebuilt Mark 2, and during the rest of the month he carried out an extended series of successful flights from the beach, often with passengers, on one occasion it

The remains of the Mark 2 at Newtownards after landing on the unexpectedly soft ground of the foreshore on 14th June 1911, the day before the Ards Agricultural Show. A cockpit seatbelt, new on the Mark 2, saved Harry, but Joe Martin was concussed and badly bruised, having been thrown violently against an upper pylon

Harry in his rebuilt
Mark 2 posing for
the photographer at
Miskelly's farm near the
shore at Newtownards
in October 1911

being a woman, although it is not recorded who this was.

Either just before or just after his return to Newtownards, Harry took his Mark 2 to his old home at Growell to demonstrate it to the family and the neighbours. He had it rigged up in the Long Field immediately to the east of the house and made ready to fly. This field is approximately 70 yards wide and runs down at a gentle incline, the 350 yards to Lough Aghery, or Ballykeel Lough as it is often called locally, which bounds the Ferguson farm to the south-east (see Appendix 12). At this point the lough narrows to about 150 yards wide and on the far side the fields rise gently for the first 50 yards or so before climbing up quite steeply to the Ballynahinch road. A local Ballykeel resident, Mr Hamilton remembers his father telling him that as a boy when he was working in the fields on the south side of the lough, word got out that Harry was about to make a flight from Growell and he dashed to a vantage point from where he could see the Long Field, just in time to see the plane rising up, crossing the lough and making a landing in Wilson's field on the south bank. This would seem the likely path a flight would have taken, as the sur- rounding terrain was not all that suitable for an aeroplane with limited capacity and manoeuvrability, due to the hazard of the lough with its soft margins, the numerous hedges incorporating trees, and the rising ground on the south side. This is the only recorded observation of a flight by Harry at Growell, but he may

well have made other flights while there, involving gentle turns and landing back in the Long Field, which was certainly adequate for take-offs and landings.

Harry may have taken his Mark 2 to Magilligan towards the end of 1911, but no record of such an event has yet been located.

Harry, in characteristic white flying suit, preparing to make a flight in his Mark 2 from the long field on the Ferguson farm at Growell in 1911

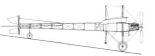

Attraction, Distraction, Instruction, Destruction

Harry shows off his Mark 2 to the family at Growell in 1911

As he entered 1912, cars and aeroplanes weren't the only things on Harry's mind. In early 1910 while he was still working at J. B. Ferguson Ltd. with brother Joe, Harry had first taken out Maureen Watson, one of the daughters of Adam Watson a prosperous grocer in Dromore, the market town for Growell. The Watsons, like the Fergusons, were Plymouth Brethren and the families were well known to each other. As the children grew up Joe and Harry both became attracted to Maureen, who had developed into a beautiful and vivacious young lady. It soon became clear that Maureen preferred Harry and, as their relationship grew stronger, Joe naturally became jealous and very frustrated. Undoubtedly this had been a contributory factor in their business split-up at the end of 1910. During 1911, whenever he could, Harry had continued the courtship with Maureen, but its path was far from easy. Not only was Harry's strongly argued agnosticism a major problem with the Watsons, as it was with his own parents, but they considered his motoring and flying exploits frivolous and inconsequential and they were far from com-

fortable with his strong personality. All in all they found him an undesirable suitor for Maureen and put every barrier they could in the way of the relationship. However with Harry's characteristic determination and Maureen's strength of feeling for him they had found ways of meeting throughout 1911 using friends and various subterfuges, and now in 1912 Harry was considering marriage and its financial implications. Although his flying enterprise was proving difficult, he still maintained a strong interest in it and he did not enjoy being defeated, but he must already have been weighing up its future potential as a business proposition. Fortunately his motor business continued to thrive and seemed certain to provide a firm basis for married life.

During 1912 Harry became involved in an increasingly pressing aspect of Ulster's political life, revolving around a Home Rule Bill for Ireland that the British government appeared to be about to introduce in Westminster. This Bill, if passed, would establish a parliament in Dublin, where the ruling majority would be Catholic. Ulster, strongly Protestant, feared that this would lead to the separation of all Ireland from Britain and the eventual destruction of the Protestant ethos in Ulster. The seem-

VAUXHALL

The car that has revolutionized the standard of automobile values. The Vauxhall is undoubtedly the best value procurable. Examine the specification of the 25 h.p. chassis and we know you will agree with us. Demonstration car sent anywhere. ——The best car in the whole world.——

Harry Ferguson Ltd.

MAY STREET, BELFAST.

Advertisement for Vauxhall cars after Harry Ferguson was granted their agency in late 1912

ingly inextricable links in Irish politics between Catholics and Nationalism, and Protestants and Loyalism meant that Harry, who most strongly believed himself to be British, felt impelled to support the Loyalist cause despite his lack of any religious belief. Ulster's political leaders, led by the eloquent and charismatic Sir Edward Carson, started a movement to exert pressure on the British government in opposition to Home Rule. Harry strongly supported the aims of the movement but initially was only involved in the background as he was not really a political animal. Later in 1914, at what was considered to be a critical time for Ulster, the political movement developed into a more militant volunteer force committed to the maintenance of Ulster's link with Britain and Harry, along with similarly committed friends owning cars, became actively involved in distributing arms to Loyalist volunteers from a cargo of guns clandestinely smuggled into the port of Larne. No doubt the challenge and the excitement of it all had a particular appeal for Harry.

The success of 'Harry Ferguson Limited' had enabled the firm to obtain several valuable motor agencies and among them was the Vauxhall agency. Vauxhall was considered one of the faster and more sporty marques at that time and these attributes were right up Harry's street, renewing his interest in competitive motoring. Soon he had a number of successes while driving Vauxhalls in local Irish trials and the Vauxhall company took notice, offering him a 3 litre works car to compete in the 1912 French Grand Prix at Dieppe on 25th and 26th June. During trials for the event his enthusiasm and competitiveness led to a near disaster. He was convinced that his car had a steering defect and he took another driver out with him on a trial run to demonstrate the problem. When travelling at around 90 mph he suddenly applied full brakes. The car left the road in a wild skid and after somersaulting twice, ended up in a ditch with its wheels in

the air. By some extraordinary chance neither of them was hurt and the car proved repairable, however during the race the car was driven by another driver. Perhaps the Vauxhall management could only take so much enthusiasm!

Meanwhile Harry's interest in aviation continued, albeit at this time in a less active way. The Aero Club of Ireland's first Irish Flying Meeting at Leopardstown in 1910 had been a great public success and had even made a profit of £400, when other similar events in England and Scotland had resulted in huge losses. Accordingly, in 1912 the Club decided it was time to organise another public event as a means of further spreading the cause of aviation in Ireland and decided on an Air Race between Dublin and Belfast. The date of 7th September was established and a prize fund of £300 was agreed. By the month of August twelve aviators had made entries, but in the event only four arrived with their aircraft. However three of them were very well known pilots, Henry Astley, Lieut. J. C. Porte and James Valentine, while the fourth was an Irishman, Desmond Arthur, who had been Cecil Grace's first passenger at the earlier Leopardstown Meeting, and full of enthusiasm, had gone on to qualify as a pilot. Once again Harry would have been level-headed enough to accept that his

Harry sitting in the 3 litre Vauxhall racing car No 54 which he was to drive in the Coupe de l'Auto at Dieppe in June 1912. This was the car that Harry crashed during a pre-race test to iron out possible steering weaknesses

Harry arranged the garaging of James Valentine's Deperdussin and Astley's Bleriot prior to the Balmoral Flying Display. The rotary engine on the Deperdussin is clearly seen, while the wheels on the Bleriot look particularly spindly

aeroplane was not yet sufficiently developed to take part. After all, the longest flight he had yet achieved would not have exceeded any more than 10 miles, and even if he had chanced his arm, he would have been competing in an underpowered aircraft of little over 35 hp, against experienced pilots in well tried machines with power ratings ranging between 50 and 100 hp. However Harry, along with John Williams, was much involved with the arrangements, particularly at the Balmoral Showgrounds just outside the Belfast boundary, where the aircraft were to finish. In the way of things, the weather on the day proved atrocious, with gale force winds and intermittent rain showers delaying the start until 4 pm, and even then only three competitors got off the ground, Desmond Arthur being swept into a flagpole during his attempted take-off. Porte in his 100 hp Deperdussin only got as far as Rathfarnham about 5 miles distant before returning to Leopardstown, explaining that even on that short flight the gusts were such that he could barely hold the control stick. Astley and Valentine both struggled gamely the 60 miles to Newry but were forced to land nearby, the very strong headwinds having reduced their fuel to the extent that they could not continue. A disappointing end to the Club's ambitious effort and a great let-down for the large crowd that had assembled at Balmoral to witness the finish of the race.

As some consolation to this hugely disappointed crowd, the Aero Club arranged for a flying display to take place at the Balmoral Showgrounds on September 14th 1912, and on this occasion Harry and John Williams were even more involved in the arrangements. All the announcements for the event were put out under Harry's name. There were to be a limited number of passenger flights at £4 4s. and £2 2s. for long and short flights respective-

117

ly, bookings to be made through 'Mr Harry Ferguson May Street'. Valentine and Astley had been commissioned to perform, and a French aviator Henri Salmet, who was at that time giving solo flying demonstrations around the Province, also agreed to take part in the display. James Valentine's machine was

Harry in discussion with James Valentine as he prepares to take off in his French Deperdussin monoplane at the Balmoral Flying Display

a Deperdussin, while Astley and Salmet both used Bleriots; all being monoplanes. Harry arranged for the garaging of Valentine's and Astley's machines when they arrived in Belfast and for their transportation to Balmoral. Despite the earlier Air Race flop a huge crowd filled the Balmoral Showgrounds and every vantage point around it. Sadly tragedy struck the meeting. During Astley's display, the engine of his Bleriot stopped without any warning and as he attempted to turn sharply away to avoid the spectators, the machine stalled into the ground with great force and he was killed instantly. This would have been the first time that Harry would have witnessed a fatal flying accident close at hand and, considering the close contact he had been having with Astley up until minutes before the accident, the shock must have been all the greater.

At the end of 1912, a year during which Harry appears to have been concentrating mostly on his motoring affairs and on his matrimonial future, an unlikely renewal of his interest in flying occurred. On Thursday 21st November a contingent of the Royal Norfolk Regiment arrived in Belfast docks and marched (over very bad roads!) to the Palace Barracks at Holywood in Co. Down. Among the contingent was a 17 year old member of the regiment's Supplementary Reserve, O. G. Lywood. As a youth of 12 years in 1907, while living near a large field that later became Gosport Airport, Lywood had become fascinated by a primitive aeroplane being built by local enthusiasts. When it proved to

James Valentine, Harry and Joe Martin inspect the remains of Astley's Bleriot after his fatal crash at the Balmoral Flying Display on 21st September 1912

be incapable of carrying the weight of an adult pilot he volunteered to have a try and was successful. Ever since this escapade he had maintained his interest in aviation, later getting further experience on a Bristol Boxkite, and when he arrived in Ulster, clearly confirming this keen interest, he immediately contacted the local flying man, Harry Ferguson, about whom he had read in the aeronautical Press. His enthusiasm won the day, although Harry probably didn't need much persuading, and on Friday 28th November Harry, John Williams, O.G. Lywood and a Mr Hartcup (probably an army colleague) set off to Magilligan with the Ferguson Mark 2. O.G.'s diary records their brief weekend there.

'Leave Belfast at 2.30 in 25 hp Vauxhall with Ferguson, Williams and Hartcup. Arrive at Magilligan 5.15, erect machine and have it ready by 11 next morning. Made quite a lot of flights with good landings. Machine not bad but in very poor condition, not really safe at all. However only went to 40 ft. She does about 50 mph. Handles quite well. Williams got some good photos. Was flying for most part of time with one burst tyre. Got back Saturday night, dead tired. Hope for some more shortly. O.G.L.'.

It is not clear whether Harry flew his aeroplane during this weekend but it would seem a little surprising if he had not made at least one flight. The comments regarding the condition of the machine are hardly surprising as there is no indication that it had been used since Harry flew it at Newtownards over a year before, in October 1911. The wish expressed by O.G. to fly the machine again was indeed fulfilled, but not until March 1913.

O.G. Lywood's initial presence in Ulster would seem to have been his annual training stint with the Royal Norfolk Regiment as a Supplementary Reserve and is likely to have been completed by Christmas 1912. It is said that O.G. at one time studied engineering in Belfast and it may be that he stayed on after his army training spell, perhaps studying at the Belfast College of Technology. After all he was only 17, although he appears to have been very advanced for his age. There is also the possibility that he worked under Harry, which could have been considered as engineering study. Whatever way it was, following the Magilligan weekend he must have discussed and agreed the further use of the aeroplane with Harry, seemingly connected with the creation of a flying school, as on 21st March 1913 he is back in Harry's May Street premises working on the Ferguson Mark 2 with John Williams and the elusive Hartcup, preparing for an early return to flying, this time at Newtownards rather than Magilligan.

O.G. Lywood flying the Mark 2 over the Back Strand at Magilligan on 28th November 1912. Harry's base, the 3-storey Point Hotel can be seen in the background

On previous flying excursions to the Newtownards area with the Ferguson aeroplane, a base had been established on Miskelly's farm more towards the eastern end of the beach. This time arrangements were made with the Gillilands of Castleavery to erect a small hangar on their foreshore land at the south-western end. Here again, access on to the beach was direct and easy, and the Comber road was less than 100 yards away along a farm lane. See map of location in Appendix 13.

Again O.G.'s diary records the activities there.

'Fri. March 21st
Worked on machine until 10.30 pm., then went to Newtownards.

John Williams' photo of the hardy participants in the brief outing of the Mark 2 at Magilligan in November 1912. Harry is on the right with O.G. Lywood beside him. O.G. holds a proper flying helmet – rather more professional than the more usual reversed flat cap, or duncher!

Sat. March 22nd
Newtownards. Machine arrived from Belfast @ 8.30 am. Worked hard all day. Cresswell & Mrs. & Dore* Mr Dunville came down in the afternoon but too much wind and machine not ready.
[*NB Cresswell, his wife and Dore are unidentified.]

Sun. March 23rd
Went to early service. Worked at machine all day.

Mon. March 24th
The school opens. Williams and self go down to shed at 4.30 am. Little wind, Williams 4 good taxis, self 2 straights @ 20 ft Hartcup several slow taxis.

Evening.
Little wind. Williams doing excellent fast rolls & off the ground several times, nearly smashed once. I made quite a lot of flights at about 3ft., with half turns and good landings. Am getting quite used to the machine. Had very bad (undecipherable) In last flight, nearly did the trick, broke four strands of one of the warping wires.

Tues. March 25th
Morning no flying as machine not ready. Evening rather a lot of wind. Ferguson did some taxis. I did a couple of flights

about 2ft, off the ground. Williams did two good taxis, breakage of inside warping wire put an end to the evening's work.

Sun. March 30th
Too windy in morning. Evening windy up to 8pm, when it went down. I went out to test and found excellent. Sent Williams for first solos. Made 4 good straights and then just after landing for the last time, suddenly opened engine full out and went up at a fearfully steep angle till he was practically vertical and then side slip and nose dive from 80ft. Nearly hit Sam* and self. Seemed dead when we first got to him, however came to a bit in about 5mins and very ill all night. Much better in a couple of days. Machine smashed to atoms. One of the worst falls I have seen, ought to have been killed. His mother watching the whole thing. Rotten luck'. [*Probably Sam Turkington.]

A contemporary report in the *Newtownards Chronicle* describing this incident states;

'The arrival this Easter time in Newtownards of a number of gentlemen interested in aviation, and the erection of a hangar on the lands of Messrs Gilliland, Castleavery, naturally aroused interest, and when it was borne home to the minds of the curious that flying was seriously intended, the slumbering embers of interest fanned into a flame, with the result that crowds congregated round the sanctum, where the eerie machine was housed, and assembled in much larger numbers on the shore edge, when it was thought that there might be a chance of flying. The efforts made by the gentlemen, who we understand were only learning the game, were by no means of a thrilling or sensational nature, most of the evolutions being confined to 'rolling' or running on the sands, although even in this we admit that a bit of nerve and confidence is required. The doyen of the visitors, a gentleman who we understand holds a pilot's certificate, did arouse some excitement by a few low-flown flights on Easter Monday, and the success of the certificated aviator was evidently sufficient to induce some of his pupils to emulate his example. Whether this is so or not, we do not pretend to know, but on Sunday evening an accident occurred to one of the aviators, who miraculously enough escaped fatal injuries. Mr Jack Williams, who we understand is associated with Mr Harry Ferguson as a director in the motor business, went out for a trial 'roll' about six o'clock. The engine was running sweetly, and Mr Williams travelled very fast over the sands, and everything seemed to be going extra well. On approaching the hangar, after a satisfactory trial, by some means the tail of the aeroplane touched the earth. This action caused the planes to elevate and, the contact giving the machine the necessary propulsion, up the aeroplane flew into the air to a height of possibly 50 ft, the engine meanwhile recording revolutions indicating a speed of over 60 miles an hour. If the machine went up quickly it came down still quicker, causing those who beheld the sight to hold their breaths, under the impression that Mr Williams must of necessity meet with fatal injuries. Happily this was not so, and he was quickly released from the entanglement of the machine. The stout strap around his waist, which keeps the aviator steady in his seat, was broken in two, and fortunately, the helmet which he wore saved him from what must have been serious injury to the head. Medical assistance was quickly requisitioned, and Dr J. Warnock and Dr D. Jamison motored, in the former's vehicle, to the scene of the occurrence, and surgical aid was immediately rendered.'

This return to Newtownards seems to have been quite an ambitious scheme by the enthusiastic O. G. to exploit Harry's aeroplane, with the backing of Harry and John Williams. It would seem that O. G's intention was to start a flying school, and that John Williams and Mr Hartcup were to be the first pupils. Although John Williams had been fully involved in all Harry's flying endeavours up to this time there is no suggestion that he had yet attempted to fly any of the aircraft, indeed, until the visit to Magilligan the previous November, when O. G. Lywood had made some flights, Harry had been the sole pilot. If things had gone better perhaps John would have been the first of many pupils, generating some return on Harry's investment, but one wonders whether the machine was sufficiently developed for training purposes. Although early aviators like Harry learnt to fly using a suck it and see technique, by this time most initial training was made in full two-seaters, often with dual controls, which were now simplified to incorporate both lateral and longitudinal control in a single joystick, rather than the two lever arrangement in the Ferguson Mark 2. If a serious attempt to establish a flying school was intended, the Ferguson Mark 2 would have needed such modifications, and it required a more powerful engine, as it was still lacking in the power necessary to cope with the extra demands of two-seat flying under training conditions, despite the improvements Harry had made to the original engine. As has been seen the method of learning had to be solo from the beginning, starting with rolls along the ground, graduating to short and long hops and eventually to full flight. Unfortunately the results were near disaster as far as the pilot was concerned, while the aeroplane was a write-off.

Harry must have been disappointed that during the visit of John Dunville, from Holywood, Co. Down, the noted balloonist and Chairman of the Aero Club of Ireland, it had not been possible to demonstrate his machine in action due to its lack of readiness and the strong winds. When Harry did his few taxi runs on the Tuesday it was the last time he would ever be at the controls of his creation, which was damaged beyond repair on the following Sunday. Apart from an abortive attempt at the resurrection of the aeroplane by Sam Turkington, who had been assisting at this last foray, the destruction of the Ferguson Mark 2 on Sunday 30th March 1913 signalled the end of Harry's flying career.

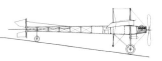

Marriage

Maureen, who played a big part in Harry's life and was his constant support

Harry got married on the 21st April 1913, the culmination of a rather contentious courtship. Not contentious in respect of his wife Maureen, who indeed was a thoroughly delightful person and deeply in love with Harry, but arising from the strict, unbending, but deeply held religious beliefs of both families. Such were the families' difficulties with the marriage that they boycotted the ceremony in the Newry Registry Office, only allowed Maureen's sister Florrie to attend after much pressure and a great deal of heartsearching. William Bell, a brother of Harry's mother who was a magistrate, and with whom Harry had always been friendly, carried out the brief ceremony. The marriage certificate was witnessed by John Lloyd Williams and Florence V. Watson, (Florrie). Despite the inauspicious beginning to their married life, their marriage proved to be long lasting and highly successful. Maureen supported Harry in every way, taking an interest in all his activities and backing him up during times of stress. Harry had periods of doubt bordering on depression and Maureen understood these moods, always being there in support. Much of Harry's future success can be attributed to the strength of Maureen's backing. Harry fully appreciated Maureen's part in his life and once said during an interview, *"A good woman is better than anything else on this earth"*.

In Retrospect

In reviewing Harry Ferguson's early adult life we can see how it was a transition from the incompatibility of farm life, through a more exciting period when he was in the thick of everything mechanical, both technically and actively, and into his first really creative phase when his inventive ability is directly linked to physical challenges and to the challenges of determination and perseverance. This aeronautical period lasted just a little over three years, and it might be said did not make a significant contribution to aviation's development overall, but it was a very considerable personal achievement, and had Harry been living in south-east England, the centre of British aviation, things are likely to have been much different, as the constant exchange of flying experience and technical knowledge amongst aviation enthusiasts could only have been beneficial, both encouraging and challenging. Harry was bitten by the bug of flying before he had ever seen an aeroplane, and yet in less than a year he had flown an aeroplane of his own design, becoming the first Irishman to do so, and indeed only the third or fourth person in the British Isles to perform similarly. His second aeroplane was a practical aircraft, well up to the standard being produced in early 1911. It was still rather under-powered and the efficiency of its controls and their manipulation needed improving, but these are not fundamental problems and could easily have been solved, indeed this is where close contact with other aviators would have been quickly beneficial. During his three years involvement in aviation Harry had put a tremendous commitment into his aeroplanes, sacrificing a considerable position with J. B. Ferguson Ltd., which must have created difficulties, and we have seen the numerous versions of his aircraft, some of them involving quite major modifications, and we have heard of his scary moments and of his injuries. There is therefore no doubt of the seriousness of his intentions during that time. In 1912 Harry needed to pay more attention to his motor business as, even then, competition was beginning to be felt, and his courtship of Maureen was now in full swing. He was nearing thirty, and perhaps by now his youthful need for physical excitement and active participation in events was on the wane, sometimes called the onset of maturity!

By 1913 his creative talents were more concentrated on the development and improvement of engines, vehicles and other mechanical equipment. Perhaps if he had continued with his aeronautics, the rapid expansion in demand for aircraft caused by the First World War would have found him a valuable part to play, but thankfully, his talents were directed towards agriculture, and this eventually resulted in a revolution in that field which benefited mankind much more fundamentally.

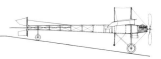

Postscript

Fig. 1 | Fig. 2

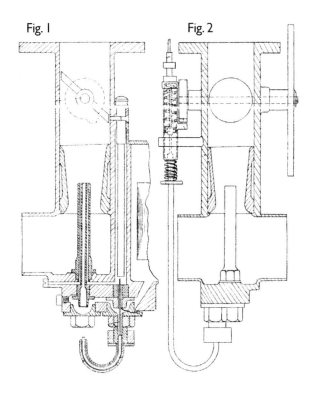

Harry's patented design for the improvement of carburettors associated with internal combustion engines

Harry Ferguson

The disastrous crash at Newtownards in early 1913, involving John Williams, left the Ferguson Mark 2 virtually a complete wreck with only the engine and pilot's seat truly worth salvaging. During 1912 Harry had been concentrating on other things and this event seems to have brought final closure to his active participation in aviation. It has been said that Maureen persuaded him to give up flying on account of the danger. All through their subsequent married life Maureen displayed total support and confidence in Harry's enterprises and it would seem unlikely that such an influence was exerted. If it was a question of danger, his car racing was just as dangerous, and in any case given his nature, trying to stop Harry was probably the best way to get him to continue. More likely, having reached the age of 29, some of his quest for excitement would have abated and he would have been drawn back to where his inherently inventive mechanical talents led, the internal combustion engine, its improvement and application. Even in 1913 these engines were relatively primitive and ripe for improvement. Harry applied his instinctive and analytical gifts to the development of more effective carburettors, essential to engine efficiency and reliability, and to better gearings, transmissions and even vehicle suspensions, taking out a number of patents related to some of these components. The approaching war led him back into agriculture and eventually along the path to his greatest achievements in tractors and ploughs, and his inspired linkage of the two. All these aspects of his later life have been fully covered in other publications.

Harry died on 25th October 1960, aged 76, at Abbotswood, his home of many years in the Cotswolds, survived by his beloved Maureen and his daughter Mrs Betty Sheldon.

John Williams

Despite his all too rapid descent at Newtownards, Williams went on to show his mettle and his commitment to flying. On 11th September 1914, just after

John Lloyd Williams in his uniform as a Lieutenant in the Royal Flying Corps after receiving his wings in July 1915

the outbreak of war he joined the Royal Engineers in Belfast. After commissioning as a 2nd Lieutenant in their Special Reserve he transferred to the Royal Flying Corps. By July 1915 he had qualified as a pilot at Netheravon on B.E.2c aircraft and on 1st August he arrived in France, where he joined No 10 Squadron also using the B.E.2c. The squadron's duties were aerial photography and artillery spotting, which were particularly hazardous operations as the slow B.E.2cs had to maintain a straight and level flight path while photographing and observing, leaving them an easy prey to the faster and more manoeuvrable German fighters. During an aerial engagement with a Fokker E1 monoplane on 26th October 1915, Williams was seriously wounded in the arm and shoulder. Losing consciousness due to lack of blood, the aircraft went out of control and his observer Lieutenant Hallam, in an extraordinary feat of bravery and skill which earned him a Military Cross, spread-eagled himself back over the fuselage and, reaching sufficiently into the rear cockpit, was able to get the aircraft down just behind the French support trenches, although it turned over violently on landing and Williams was thrown out. Hallam managed to climb out and, although wounded himself in his left hand which he later lost, assisted Williams until help arrived. (see Appendix 14 for Combat Report details). Williams remained in the 4th General Hospital in Versailles until taken off the danger list in November, returning on convalescent leave to England in December. After a period of recovery and re-posting in England during 1916, he was sent to Canada to train new pilots at RFC Camp Borden in Ontario, remaining there until the end of the war in 1918. He was commissioned Captain in the newly formed Royal Air Force in December 1918 and after demobilisation he returned to Ulster and to Harry Ferguson Ltd., where henceforth he was always referred to affectionately as Cap by the staff and workers alike, giving some indication of his straightforward and pleasant personality and the general respect for him. During the '20s and '30s, as Harry developed his tractors and ploughs and their production, John Williams was his right hand man in all his business transactions in the UK and in the USA, and his staunch friend at every turn.

At the outbreak of the Second World War, John Williams immediately rejoined the RAF, being gazetted in the RAF Volunteer Reserve as a Pilot Officer on 14th September 1939. Tragically, a year later almost to the day on 11th September 1940, he was killed in a traffic accident near Morcambe in Lancashire under black-out conditions. At that time he held the rank of Flight Lieutenant.

So died Harry's greatest friend and valued colleague, a colleague who had worked with him right through the difficult '30s, and now when the Ferguson tractors and their integrated systems were at last into production he was not there to enjoy the satisfaction of success. As a gesture of his loss, Harry donated the entire cost of a Spitfire to the *Belfast Telegraph's* then running Spitfire Fund, but this was just a superficial outward expression of his deep sense of personal loss, a sense of loss he retained throughout the rest of his life.

O.G. Lywood

Made his brief but dynamic arrival into Harry's life just at the end of its aeronautical phase, and returned to England after the accident at Newtownards to continue his flying activities there, being granted Pilot's Licence No. 600 by the Royal Aero Club of the UK on 21st August 1913. As a 2nd Lieutenant in their Supplementary Reserve, he joined his regiment the Royal Norfolk Regiment at the outbreak of the First World War. With his experience of flying he was soon attached to the Royal Flying Corps and was sent to France with No 9 Squadron, an early wireless telegraphy unit tasked to put to use this form of communication between aircraft and the ground, affording a more effective transfer of information between observers and the army below. He was posted to the squadron's HQ Section at St. Omer, where among his fellow officers was J. T. C. Moore-Brabazon, now a lieutenant in the RFC. Moore-Brabazon

Photograph of Oswyn George (O.G.) Lywood on his Aviator's Certificate No 600, granted by the Royal Aero Club of the United Kingdom on 21st August 1913

later recalled this squadron's officers as being, *'a collection of the most brilliant officers he had ever met'*. In order to take a more active role in the RFC, Lywood went through its pilot training course, although already the holder of a Civil Licence, and on completion returned to France, eventually rising to command a squadron, before being wounded and grounded. By the end of the war he held the rank of major and in 1919 was offered a permanent commission, serving in India throughout the '20s and mid '30s when he returned to England and was appointed to the Air Ministry. By the time war broke out he was Director of Signals at the Air Ministry, where in 1941 he played a leading part in ensuring that all fighter aircraft were fitted with the new VHF radios, essential to their success and safety. From 1942 until 1946 he was Air Officer Commanding No 26 Group RAF. John Terraine, in his history of the RAF during the Second World War, identifies Lywood as one of the 11 men who were true fathers of weapons vital to the RAF. He retired in 1946 as an Air Vice Marshall with the honours of C.B. and C.B.E. He died in 1957 at Woodland, near Sevenoaks in Kent.

Joe Martin's car and cycle business premises at 18 Princes Street, Dromore c. 1906. Joe stands in the centre with his father, Alexander, to his right. Note the bare car chassis awaiting their custom-built bodies by local coachbuilders

Joe Martin

Harry's longest serving working assistant was born at Lagan Ballyroney just outside Dromore in 1887. He had a mechanical bent and soon after leaving school opened up a small bicycle shop at 18 Princes Street, Dromore. Although started as a bicycle shop it later handled motorcycles and light cars as can be seen in the attached trade photograph, which shows Joe standing proudly outside his shop with his father and three assistants. (Visited 100 years later it was a delight to see that it remains today exactly as it was then, even to the curtains on the upstairs windows!) During 1906, as has been described, Joe Ferguson planned the move to new prestige premises in Chichester Street, Belfast to cater for the expanding business of J. B. Ferguson Ltd., moving there in June 1907. It had become known that additional skilled staff were being sought to cater for this increase in business and it is not surprising, with the company's high reputation and its local family connection in the Dromore area, that Joe Martin sold his business to a local man Mr Magill and went to work for the Fergusons. Joe started with them in Little Donegall Street in early 1907 just before the move to Chichester street. During Joe's time working in Dromore he had acquired a considerable range of mechanical experience and he was a born engineer; thoughtful, precise and hard working, so he was a valuable asset to the company. One particular expertise he had, especially useful in the early days of his service when the roads were so poor, was in the construction and repair of wheels. Later when Harry made some heavy landings this skill was called upon again. Joe helped on the construction of Harry's first aeroplane in Chichester Street and was involved at Hillsborough in all the flight trials. When Harry started up on his own Joe went with him to May Street motors, working on the construction of the Ferguson Mark 2 and assisting at most of its outings until at least June 1911, when he was injured in Harry's landing accident, and almost certainly in October of that year when Harry made his last full flights in it at Newtownards. Although Joe could turn his hand to any demands thrown up by Harry's day to day motor business, he was very much identified with all aspects of the aeroplanes and gave great assistance to Harry during his flying activities when a practical and adaptive mechanic was invaluable, one able to cope with the varied and urgent repairs often needed.

In the early days of setting up on his own in May Street, Harry visited many of the car manufacturers in England and Scotland to inspect their products and to try to obtain agencies. On a number of these trips he took Joe Martin along to benefit from his practical engineering knowledge before coming to any decisions and Joe recalled in an interview in 1965, that they visited the Star factory in Wolverhampton, the Vauxhall works in Luton, the Bean works in Tipton and the Austin works in Birmingham, where they met Sir Herbert Austin the pioneer car manufacturer. He also recalled that following the grant of the Star agency, he drove the first of their cars to arrive in Belfast from the docks to the garage in May street, and indeed, the first car sold from May street was a Star.

Joe got married in 1913 and as far as is known remained in Belfast working for Harry Ferguson Ltd., as the firm was now called, until about 1920 when he returned to Dromore to work as senior plant engineer for the very large civil engineering contractors, Grahams of Dromore. During his thirty or so years with Grahams he was responsible for the maintenance of their heavy plant and he developed many practical mechanical devices and

accessories to improve their working. He also took on the training of apprentice mechanics and one of these, another Dromore
man Sam Cherry, said of him, "Joe worked us hard and did not
put up with any nonsense. But he was a brilliant mechanic. If
there was no tool to do a particular job he just set to and made
one".

Joe lived in 34 Mount Street, close to Grahams main works in
Dromore and retired in 1952 aged 65, although in retirement he
kept busy, often helping out friends and neighbours in practical ways. During Harry Ferguson's later life he returned often to
Ulster on holidays, visiting old friends and places, increasingly to
reminisce. On these visits he always called with Joe to talk over
old times, on one occasion presenting him with a car. This gives
some measure of Harry's appreciation of all Joe's work and support during his early business life. Joe Martin died at the ripe old
age of 93 in 1979, but not before he had been able to advise on
the construction of the replica Ferguson Mark 2 as previously
described.

Leslie Wilkinson

His life is less well documented than that of Joe Martin but he
also played a long and important part in Harry's activities during
the early business years. Almost certainly from the Hillsborough
area he operated a bicycle shop in Main Street, Hillsborough
during the years 1901-1908. He took an early interest in the
internal combustion engine and by late 1904 had acquired a
Riley motorcycle. Riding this machine he finished third in a Hill
Climb at Gilnahirk organised by the Ulster Centre of the MCUI
in April 1905. In their next event, a 100 mile Reliability Trial
from Belfast to Dundalk and back in June, he rode a Minerva
motorcycle, possibly acquired through J. B. Ferguson Ltd. Both
he and Harry finished well but were disqualified for getting off
and pushing their bikes up a steep hill! In July he took part, again
on a Minerva, in the Ulster Centre's 400 mile 2-day Reliability
Trial for their newly acquired Muratti Cup; Belfast to Dublin
and back on the first day and Belfast to Derry and back on the
second. He came third in this gruelling event, no mean performance at the time. There is no record of Leslie Wilkinson's cycle

shop in Hillsborough after 1908 and Leslie was at Hillsborough Large Park in November and December 1909 assisting Harry during his first flight trials and his first flight. It would seem likely that he joined J. B. Ferguson Ltd. in Chichester Street in late 1908 or early 1909. Unlike Joe Martin's wide engineering ability, Leslie's expertise was more specifically as a motor mechanic, although clearly a talented one, as Harry himself was very knowledgeable and very particular in this respect. It is likely that, under Harry's direction, Leslie would have been the one who carried out the actual modifications to the JAP aero engine in early 1911 to improve its efficiency. When Harry was taking part in Irish Trials in Vauxhall cars during 1911 and in early 1912, Leslie was his mechanic and sometimes riding mechanic if this was permitted or called for. It has not been possible to trace Leslie's progress after this time.

Sam Turkington

Turkington's name first appears at the time when the Ferguson Mark 2 is being checked over by O. G. Lywood and being taken back to Newtownards in early 1913. It would seem likely therefore that he joined Harry Ferguson Ltd. in 1912, although no information on his background has yet been identified. Sam was probably a fitter rather than a specialist motor mechanic, as after the crash involving John Williams he took over the shattered remains of the machine intending to rebuild and fly it again, which would have required wider construction skills. Harry accepted Sam's intentions and gave him the use of the JAP engine as encouragement. However it was not long before Sam realised the difficulties and costs involved in the enterprise and gave up the idea, returning the engine to Harry. Details of Sam Turkington's later career are not known.

Appendices

Appendix 1: The Ferguson Children

1. Joseph Bell Ferguson   born 24th May 1880.
2. James Patterson Ferguson   born 18th June 1881
3. Maggie Elizabeth Ferguson   born 19th May 1883
4. Henry George Ferguson (Harry)   born 4th November 1884
5. Mary Agnes Ferguson   born 1st December 1886
6. Norman Priestly Ferguson   born 3rd March 1888
7. William Edwin Persis Ferguson   born 27th October 1890
8. Sarah Ludley Agnew Ferguson   born 26th August 1891
9. John Victor Stanley Ferguson   born 2nd September 1893
10. Edgar McKnight Ferguson   born 16th July 1896
11. Hugh Fisher Ferguson   born 28th November 1903

Appendix 2: Letter from Harry Ferguson to Ireland's Saturday Night in response to the comment in their report on the Gilnahirk hill climb on 22nd September 1906 that, 'the first three finishers were clearly too liberally treated by the handicapper'.

'Referring to the report of the Gilnahirk hill climb in the last edition of the Ireland's Saturday Night, commenting on the result, your reporter makes the statement that the winners were far too liberally dealt with. Now, this is most misleading, and I regret that I cannot allow it to pass without saying a word in my defence. It is also, surely, a slight on the gentlemen who so kindly, and I have no doubt, so accurately worked out the handicap. So far as my own handicap was concerned, I was allowed 12.2/5 secs. on the scratch man, but there were 6 secs. taken off this, as a penalty for previous wins this season, which gave me 6.2/5 secs. from the scratch man. This, I think, is just and fair, and if I had been put back scratch I would have competed all the same and done my best to win - as I always do. There is no person I can assure you, who does more for the Union than myself, and I can can easily grasp the fact that it would not be for its benefit that one man wins all the time. I do not desire this, but what I desire is that when I make a fair performance (and you will yourself admit that Saturday's was by no means a bad one on a standard 2 ¾ hp Machine) that it is not made light of. Of course, I am well aware of the fact that every competitor has not the same facilities for putting his machine in order for such a contest as this as I myself have, and with this in view, I do not object in the least being penalised. At the same time, I think that you will yourself agree with me that the man who gives his machine the most attention and does not leave the merest detail undone that will give him a few seconds, is the man who should win, other things being equal. Trusting that I have not taken up too much of your time, and that you will see your way to publish this letter, or make my points clear in the next issue of your widely- circulated and interesting paper".

Appendix 3: *Ireland's Saturday Night's* reply in their 29th September 1906 issue to Harry Ferguson's letter with regards to handicapping:

The observation to which he takes exception is in fact that the three placed men were too liberally treated by the handicapper. That surely is a matter for the handicapper rather than for Mr Ferguson, and I do not see where the latter has any grounds for complaint. What I object to is the fact that handicappers generally follow a cast iron system, based upon the stroke and bore of the engine and the weight of the rider. That is a system that ought to be altered, because it has over and over again been proved to be unjust to the general body of the competitors by reason of the fact that expert mechanical geniuses like Mr Ferguson can so 'doctor' a machine as to make the issue absolutely safe on such a basis. The Gilnahirk contest is only another proof of this. It is quite true that this 'doctoring' is not prohibited by the rules, but it places all machines not so improved at a great disadvantage, for which allowance ought to be made in the handicap if the contest is to have even a semblance of fairness.

It so happens that the report objected to was written by me, so that I am in a position to defend it. The allegation that it is misleading ought to be substantiated by some evidence as to its error, but this has not been done for the very obvious reason that the facts make it impossible to do so. So far from this allegation being true it is the very reverse. What can be juster than to give his own statement as to the horsepower of his engine, the actual time occupied in covering the distance and the handicap allowance? Do not these facts set out in the truest light the actual position and so set it out as to show that Mr Ferguson won, yet presumably because a fulsome compliment has been added he describes this as misleading. It is nothing to the point at issue to offer to the handicapper the wholly unnecessary compliment that he has 'kindly and accurately worked out the handicap'. I have as high an appreciation of his kindliness and accuracy upon the formula as Mr Ferguson and neither of these qualities do I attack. The point I make is that the formula upon which he – in common with other handicappers proceeds – does not attain the desired result, because experts like Mr Ferguson are able to defeat it and give themselves an advantage inaccessible to others. The whole object of a handicapper, as I understand it, is to bring the entire of the competitors within the smallest compass of time or of distance at the finish of the contest, and any handicap that fails to accomplish this is not a good one. Has the handicap in question achieved this? The answer is the official times returned, which disclose that even after the handicap allowance has been deducted some of the competitors are separated from Mr Ferguson by twenty seconds, almost equal to one half of the time occupied by the winner in covering the whole distance. Not a single one of the other six competitors was anywhere within measurable distance of the three placed men, and to speak of such a handicap as 'just and fair' is simply a 'short circuit' of the truth. A handicap to be effective and fair ought to give an allowance equivalent to the differences in speed of the machines handicapped, and if it is found that these machines simply run away with an event is it any exaggeration to say that they have been too liberally treated by the handicapper? Doesn't the fact speak for itself?

My view is that a handicapper, instead of adhering to a rigid system, ought to exercise judicial discretion where he has judicial knowledge of facts that ought properly be considered. The moment the handicap was made known everyone was aware that the issue lay only between Mr Ireton and Mr Ferguson; in fact Mr Ferguson admitted this himself to me on the morning of the contest. I notice that he describes his motorcycle as a standard 2¾ hp machine. His definition must be pretty elastic. Does he pretend that the machine as he rode it, was a standard pattern just as it left the maker's hands, and as any other person will receive by ordering a 'standard pattern?' I am sure he will not give an affirmative answer, and if he did he would be grossly inaccurate, for it is now different from the standard as much as a thoroughbred horse differs from a good hackney, and it therefore ought to be handicapped correspondingly and not as if it were a standard pattern as he received it.

His suggestion that the performance he has accomplished has been made light of I do not understand. The whole point of my complaint is quite the other way, and for that reason I contend that all three winners accomplished such fast times that they ought to have been more heavily handicapped, simply because on the handicap not one of the others had a ghost of a chance. It is not conductive to the general good of the sport to ask nine or ten others to enter and pay a fee for the mere privilege of riding over, while two or three carry out a contest entirely farcical as far as the rest are concerned.

I quite appreciate his keen interest in the sport, although I can hardly go as far as to subscribe to the egotism in which he has indulged. I am quite sure he will compete, no matter what his mark may be, and as a man of the trade, that is good business. Coming from him, the suggestion that his performance has been studiously belittled is peculiarly offensive, for he must know that there is not only no foundation for such an opinion, but everything to favour of the contrary view. Although the firm he represents do not advertise with this paper, I wrote an appreciation of the manner in which one of their machines had behaved in the Muratti trophy contest which he thought worthy of reproducing on a page advertisement in some of the trade organs. A little reflection will, I think make it clear to Mr Ferguson that he has no grievance whatsoever and has no injustice done to him; until he has, it is scarcely worth while to conjure up imaginary wrongs and impute motives where none exist. As a business man he will recognise that he cannot, under the guise of correspondence expect a free advertisement and it is my business to prevent any such attempt, although I have relaxed the rule in this case".

Appendix 4: Report in Ireland's Saturday Night of 24th August on controversy regarding the tied result in the 1907 Muratti trophy and subsequent objections by the two participants, Harry Ferguson and James Stewart.

There are one or two matters in connection with the Muratti Trophy contest which, though still sub-judice, I propose to discuss at this stage. My reason for departing from my usual practice and doing so now is the fact that mis-statements have been circulated, which totally misrepresent the facts of the case. Mr Harry Ferguson, as my readers will be aware, tied this year for the trophy with Mr James Stewart, and the Committee after full considerations of all the facts, directed these two to make a further day's reliability run over the Belfast to Derry and back course. Their machines having in the meantime been impounded from the conclusion of the trial proper. Mr Ferguson declined to act on the direction, and on the morning following the decision removed his machine from the 'control', and wrote a letter to the public Press declining to further compete for the trophy, as he claimed to have 'already and beyond dispute won it', adding, 'My reasons for adopting this attitude are and were last night known to the Committee'. Mr Ferguson has, in fact, according to his version, been ruthlessly martyred by the Committee, in which, curious to say, two of his own personal friends sat, and concurred in the course taken. Someone on his behalf 'stuffed' the cycling writer of a contemporary with a similar fairy tale of his grievances, and this week I had the opportunity of seeing the draft copy of a letter which Minerva Motors Ltd., have sent to the Trade Press, presumably on information supplied by, or on behalf of, Mr Ferguson, in which a laudable stand is made on behalf of 'honesty and fair play', and the usual rhodomontade [vain boasting] of that kind peculiar to the trade, who preach lofty sporting morality but set few examples of the same.

In these circumstances I deem it a duty to set out in extenso the facts, and allow the public to judge of the 'honesty, fair play and sporting spirit' of the transactions. When the returns from all the 'open controls' were made it was seen four riders had tied with full marks. The returns from the 'secret controls' were then worked out, and it was found that Stewart and Ferguson again tied with 2,165 points each. So far all parties were agreed. I happened to have been in the chair on the occasion of this meeting, and I made the suggestion that each should have possession of the trophy for six months or that a further round should be ridden off to find the winner. Mr Ferguson refused to act upon either suggestion, and then proceeded to lodge two objections to Stewart. First, that he had made some repairs to his machine while in control in Belfast on the second day of the contest, and secondly, that he had slipped off his belt and drained the oil from his crank case while in control at Limavady. Stewart countered this by lodging a protest against Ferguson for adjusting his commutator, and permitted his mechanic to attempt to true up a wheel that had got twisted.

Ferguson's protests were first considered. On the first charge he could not call any corroboration whatever, and he admitted that though over half a dozen persons were present on the alleged occasion he made no protest against what was being done to any person present. Stewart gave the most positive denial to the statement, and affirmed that in no way had he touched his machine in Belfast. Under these conditions that count of the protest was dismissed. Stewart admitted that he had drained oil out of his crank case, and that he had slipped off the belt and put it on again, but stated that this was done before he had handed in his card, and secondly he denied that it was either an 'adjustment' or a repair according to rule. The accuracy of the first statement was admitted. Upon the second point there was a precedent. A protest had been decided two years ago on this very question, so that the committee were again left with no alternative but to cast this protest also. Stewart's protest then came on, but he stated that he regarded both Ferguson's protest and his own as contemptible and unsportsmanlike, and had only entered his as a counter to Ferguson's, and would now not proceed with it, and across the table he made on the spot a friendly challenge to decide the issue either by a hill climb, a speed trial, or a reliability run. But Mr Ferguson was not 'having any'. This 'injured innocent', who only wants fair play and honest dealing, pushed his protest to the bitter end, and was unable either upon the facts or upon the rules to sustain it, while his opponent withdrew a protest which upon the evidence that has now come to light could not have been resisted, for two witnesses on Tuesday night last came forward in answer to subsequent protests by Mr Ferguson against other riders who pledged themselves to this statement that Mr Ferguson had in control cleaned and adjusted his commutator, and his mechanic had been in the attempt to true up a wheel and was ordered to desist.

As Mr Ferguson refused to ride over in compliance with the decision – the absolutely unanimous decision – of this committee, the trophy was awarded to Mr Stewart. Subsequently Mr Ferguson lodged protests against three other riders, which were to have been investigated on Tuesday night last, of which fact he had notice. Without so much as a word of explanation to anyone he left town on Monday night, and did not even send a line in support of his protest, with the result that one gentleman had to travel all the way from London to defend a protest that was purely figmentary, and was not proceeded with by the man who made it. The committee would have been perfectly justified there and then in coming to a decision, but they have on the contrary allowed the matter to remain over for a fortnight in order that he may have the fullest opportunity to substantiate his own and make answer to the others. As 'sporting spirit and honesty' have been introduced into this matter, I think it right to mention that at the committee meeting one member asserted that canvassing had been resorted to on behalf of Mr Ferguson, and stated that he himself had been approached on the subject. I had, as chairman, to request Mr Ferguson, as a member of the committee, to refrain from voting upon his own protest, so that the less said about 'sporting spirit' the better. Those are the facts of the case, and it is upon them that Mr Ferguson 'claims to have already and beyond dispute won'. The validity of the claim will be judged by the public as it has already been by the committee. I am sure the writer in a contemporary would not willingly do anything unfair to anyone, he now knows the whole facts, and I feel sure he will put the truth candidly to the public. As to Minerva Motors, whose machine Mr Ferguson rode, I shall see that a copy of this paper reaches them. Their game obviously is an advertisement free if possible. Let them have it by all means, but they have no right to give currency to erroneous statements casting a grave reflection upon a sporting body. The fact is that Mr Ferguson has been treated with consideration quite beyond the merits of the case, and he would do well to bear in memory the fact that there are men left still in sport whose 'sporting spirit and fairness' will bear comparison with his. I know no man who is capable of getting better results out of a machine, he has done many fine performances in his time, and will, I hope, do many more. His reputation as an expert is at the very highest, but it will not be enhanced by launching utterly groundless charges at a committee of which he is himself a member, nor will his repute as a sportsman be enlarged by the attempt to capture a trophy through the medium of protests which he cannot sustain either on facts or rules, and some of which he does not even come forward to support.

It is difficult to understand the extent to which Harry took his protests on this occasion. We know of his competitiveness, and can believe that initially he clearly considers that he won the event, but in the light of the disclosures and discussions in the committee, of which he was a member, one would have thought that sharing the trophy was the sensible thing to do. However, Harry had a stubborn streak and was not one to back down, and he simply walks away in high dudgeon, a mood that may perhaps have been aggravated by the apparently difficult relationship, previously alluded to, that he shared with the correspondent/reporter of the *Ireland's Saturday Night,* who was also the chairman of the committee.

Appendix 5: Map showing locations of various Ferguson properties in Belfast

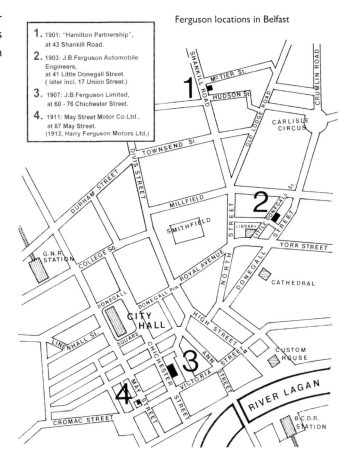

1. 1901: "Hamilton Partnership", at 43 Shankill Road.
2. 1903: J.B.Ferguson Automobile Engineers, at 41 Little Donegall Street. (later incl. 17 Union Street.)
3. 1907: J.B.Ferguson Limited, at 60 - 76 Chichester Street.
4. 1911: May Street Motor Co.Ltd., at 87 May Street. (1912, Harry Ferguson Motors Ltd.)

Ferguson locations in Belfast

Appendix 6: Creative Timescale from initial interest to first flight.

1908 Aug to Dec	Wilbur Wright in France making first public demonstrations of true controlled flight. Considerable coverage of his flights given in the National Press.
1909 25th July	Bleriot crosses English Channel. Great international impact and extensive publicity.
26th July to 20th Aug	Harry and John Williams greatly interested in this exciting new form of transport. Study the new *Flight* magazine. Decide to build an aeroplane.

21st to 31st Aug	They attend world's first International Flying Meeting at Rheims. Watch aircraft flying. Make notes and sketches of aircraft. Talk to aviators.
1st to 22nd Sept	Consider information gathered at Rheims. Assess design options. Sketch tentative ideas.
23rd Sept to 4th Oct	Attend Paris Aero Salon. Make detailed study of exhibits. (Harry tells reporter of intentions to build plane, but no drawings yet prepared).
5th Oct to 16th Nov	Harry's stated six week design and construction period: Prepare basic drawings. Set up construction area in mezzanine at back of Chichester Street premises. Start construction. Green engine arrives but is damaged beyond repair during testing. Study interlude at Blackpool Flying Meeting, 18th to 25th Oct. (incl. travel time) construct. JAP engine arrives. Beedle propeller arrives. Fuselage and wings moved to part of motor showroom in the ground floor of Chichester Street premises, to permit full assembly of aeroplane. Mark 1 aeroplane ready for dispatch to Hillsborough.
17th to 27th Nov	First trials at Hillsborough. Mark 1 aeroplane proves unsatisfactory. Return to Chichester Street (incl. travel times).
28th Nov to 12th Dec	Modifications made to aeroplane. Main undercarriage simplified. Second upper to cabane pylon fitted. 'New' set of wings provided (see note below). Now Mark 1A.
13th to 30th Dec	Second flight trials at Hillsborough (incl. travel times) to Mark 1A aircraft, initially fitted with Beedle propeller has poor results. Later fitted with Cochrane propeller, it performs better. A number of short hops and very brief flights carried out.
31st Dec	First proper flight.

Appendix 7: Location of the first flight within Hillsborough Large Park.

Little definitive information has been recorded or handed down on the precise location of Harry's first flight within the Large Park.

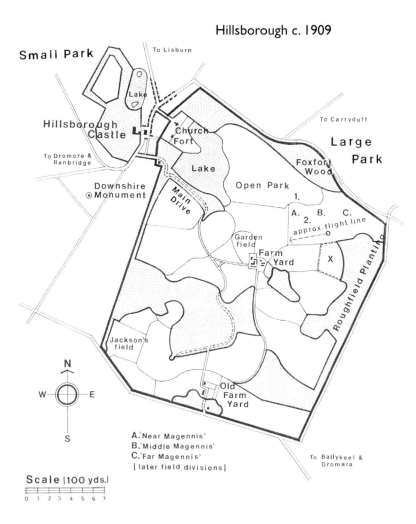

Hillsborough c. 1909

Small Park

To Lisburn

Hillsborough Castle

Lake

To Dromore & Banbridge

Church Fort

Lake

To Carryduff

Large Park

Foxford Wood

Downshire Monument

Main Drive

Open Park

1.

A.   B.   C.
2.
approx. flight line

Garden field

Farm Yard

X

Roughfield Planting

Jackson's field

N

W ⊕ E

S

Old Farm Yard

A. 'Near Magennis'
B. 'Middle Magennis'
C. 'Far Magennis'
[later field divisions]

To Ballykeel & Dromara

Scale (100 yds.)
0 1 2 3 4 5 6 7

In an attempt to resolve the question, the author has visited the Large Park on two occasions, on the first visit getting a most helpful conducted tour by the present Farm Manager, Mr Morrison, and on the second occasion being taken to a specific location called Jackson's Field on the south-west corner of the Park by Robert Ballagh, a life long employee and resident on the Estate farm, now retired. A study was made of several Ordnance Maps dated as close as possible to 1909. Original photographs of the Ferguson aeroplanes at Hillsborough were examined closely in conjunction with the maps and compared with information gleaned on the above site visits, and with photographs taken during them.

The maps, dated 1858, 1903 and 1919, show surprisingly little change even today, from the original landscaping of the Park as planned by Lord Trevor Hillsborough in the early

145

1700s and carried on by his son Lord Wills. Today approximately half of the 1000 acre Large Park is farmed. In 1909 a little more of the area was clear of plantations, as the Open Park to the east of the lake had not yet been planted out. Clearly the plantations have been managed, as trees are cut down due to old age or disease or for their timber, but their overall visual appearance from the open ground is still quite recognisable. The open ground of the Park had fewer field divisions in the early 1900s, and these can be seen on the Hillsborough map elsewhere in the main body of the script. In more recent times some fields have been divided up, and given names for convenient reference, such as Near, Middle and Far Magennis (A, B, and C) on the map, and one relevant field in the far south western corner of the Park is known as Jackson's Field, although it may have had that name from earlier times.

In 1909 there were only two vehicular accesses into the Park. The main one was located just to the south of the Town Square as it is today, the second entrance being off the Dromara Road in the south wall of the Park at what was even then called the Old Farm Yard. The driveway from the main entrance weaved through the planting at the south-west of the lake, as it still does, and curved round to the Farm Yard which is now the core of the Agricultural Research Station. There were estate pathways between the Farm Yard and the Old Farm Yard and to various fields, but these were only designed for farm workers and horses and other livestock, or for horse drawn carts and basic farm machinery at best.

The only information on the location of Harry's first flights in the Park that have come to light up to the time of writing comes from Robert Ballagh, who came to the Park as a young boy when his father took up employment and residence at the farm in the 1940s. Robert himself also lived and worked there until his retirement. Robert recalls that the tradition among Park employees was that Harry flew in Jackson's Field, mentioned above. This field is clearly large enough, being approximately 300 yards square and, while it is reasonably level north-south, it has a considerable cross fall west-east. Jackson's Field is tucked away in a relatively remote part of the park, and this might have been an attraction, although Harry cannot be considered as being at all secretive. Harry's first aeroplanes were completed in Chichester Street, Belfast and towed on their own wheels to Hillsborough. If Jackson's Field was used, access would probably have been made via the Old Farm Yard entrance, as its present direct entrance from the Dromara Road at its south-western corner is a later provision. The aeroplane would then have been manhandled across to Jackson's Field and the wings attached there. This procedure would have been relatively easy, and in later outings of his various machines was often the case. There is one rather poor, touched up newspaper photograph of the Mark 1 sitting on open ground with a tree plantation in the background, similar to that on the western boundary of Jackson's Field. However the aeroplane is sitting in a very slight hollow relative to the photographer, with the ground rising only slightly towards the trees beyond. Jackson's field however, rises fairly steeply all the way upwards to the trees on its boundary. It would therefore seem unlikely that the location of this particular photograph of the very first machine is in Jackson's field. This of course cannot rule out the use of that field, and handed down information often has a basis of truth. However Robert Ballagh himself, while reporting this as quite a strongly held tradition, readily agreed that it was by no means a certainty, and if the same photograph is compared with a location (1) on the Open Park looking towards the Foxfort Wood, there seems to be a reasonable match. In any case, the Mark 1 did not achieve proper flight and we therefore have to consider the case of the successful Mark 1A.

The Mark 1A, arriving as before from Belfast, almost certainly used the main driveway to the Farm Yard, as there is a front view photograph of the Mark 1A clearly taken soon after erection, which includes both the Downshire Monument and the Hillsborough Church spire, enabling the location to be established as, in or near the field just west of the Farm Yard known then, and now, as the Garden Field. The use of the relatively sheltered farm yard area, with possible access to a farm shed, makes this a logical and desirable base for Harry's trials, as it must always be remembered that it was mid winter.

The next photograph of the Mark 1A is a good three quarter rear view of it and was clearly taken around the same time as the frontal view, as the same personnel in the same clothing are posing with the aeroplane and there is snow upon the ground. In the background there is a substantial planting on rising ground which is fronted by a scrubby area with some sparse hedging and signs that some small trees have been cut down. The only location in the Park around 1909 that appears to fit this combination of a planting with rough growth in front, seems to be the Roughfield Planting on the eastern boundary of the Park, which at that time had a designated rabbit warren in front of it, marked X. Although it was an overcast winter day, there are slight highlights from the sun on the faces of Harry and an adjoining man which would tie in with late afternoon winter sun if the Mark 1A is positioned as suggested at this location, marked 2 on the map. At that time it would have been in a very large field extending to the eastern corner of the Park. Today it would be in a subdivided portion of that field, nowadays referred to as The Near Magennis, marked A.

The photograph showing the Mark 1A in motion just off the ground, although not taken on the first flight, is probably on one of the long hops leading up to that event and close to where it took place. The same planting as in the three quarter photograph is in the background of this one, and the rabbit warren area is even more clearly seen. Again it is suggested that this location is in The Near Magennis, although in a slightly different position and orientation.

Summary

This rather heavyweight – and perhaps unnecessary – study convinces the writer at least, that the flight trials all took place in the area including the present Near and Middle Magennis fields and the upper part of the Open Park near Foxfort Wood, and that the actual first flight of the Mark 1A started in the then unnamed big field, at its highest point, now in Middle Magennis, near the then rabbit warren at Roughfield Planting, and going down towards the Garden Field over the Near Magennis part of the big field.

Appendix 8: Map showing Magilligan where Harry tested Mark ID.

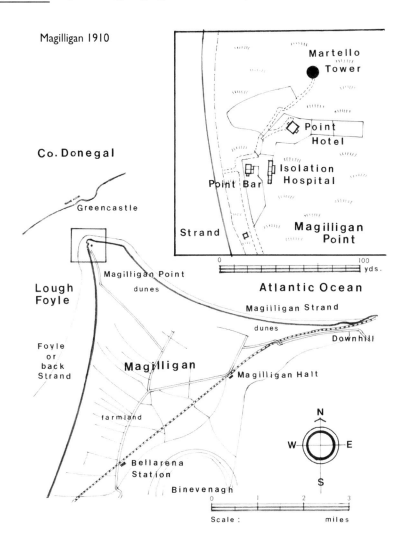

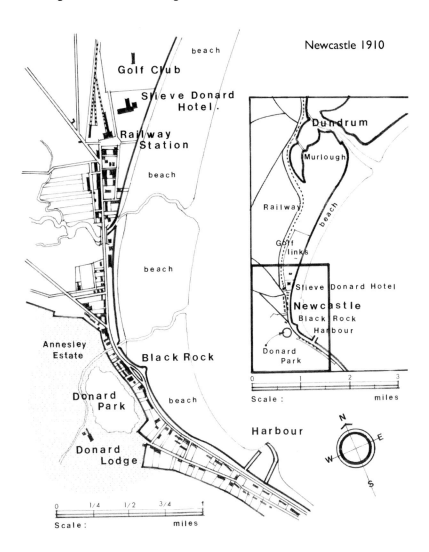

Appendix 10: View showing wing attachments and pilot's controls on the Mark 2

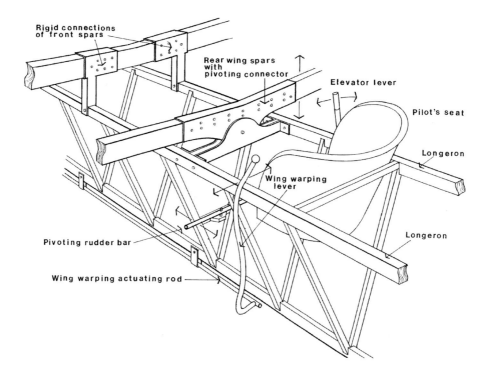

Appendix 11: Article *How I Made a 35 hp Engine Go* by Harry Ferguson in the January 11th 1912 issue of *The Aeroplane*.

'There must be a large number of 35 hp JAP air-cooled engines lying unused in aeroplane sheds all over the country. I believe this to be one of the most substantially-built engines on the market, and I am confident, if their owners took pains to get over the several minor troubles which these engines are subject to, they would find that they really had an excellent engine to work with. I cannot think of any engine that would be more economical to run or more reliable for school work, and I have no hesitation in saying that if these engines were fished out of their sheds, and alterations made to them which I have made to mine, that we should hear a lot more about them and see them in use daily.

The things which, in my opinion, completely spoil this otherwise excellent engine are: Firstly, overheating after about seven minutes' running. Secondly, the flow of oil into the pilot's face, making flight almost impossible. Thirdly, the low horse-power developed by the engine after it has been running a few minutes, consequent on overheating. Fourthly, the danger of fire. Fifthly, the fact that the engine will not turn slowly.

When flying with my machine at Magilligan last year I always found that after five to seven minutes' flight the pistons would run perfectly dry, and this would be the case no matter how much oil I started off with in my crank case or how much I let run into the cylinders by the usual JAP Methods.

Of course, with dry pistons no engine will keep cool, and I quickly came to the conclusion that the overheating was entirely due to bad lubrication, and that the bad lubrication was due to the open ports in the cylinders letting the oil escape. There are lots of ways of closing up auxiliary ports, but the best way I found, after experimenting, was to tap the holes in the cylinders with a very fine thread and then screw slightly tapered plugs into the holes, taking full advantage of the depth of the thread by letting the plug go in as far as it could without touching the piston.

When I had all these plugs screwed in I ran a saw-mark round them, and then put a piece of wire round the groove thus made to keep them from screwing out. This, however, was hardly necessary, owing to the fact that when the engine gets hot the plugs get tighter.

I then fitted a set of exhaust pipes, which carried the exhaust gas, and any oil that might be going, clear of the machine. I was well aware that these alterations would necessitate my making many more important alterations to the engine, because these open ports play a very important part in filling up the cylinders on the induction stroke and in letting the gas away on the exhaust stroke.

To make certain that there would be no possibility of the gas being choked going into the engine I went over all the inlet passages from the valves right out to the crown piece in the centre of the inlet pipes; I made more room past the inlet guides, and rounded off the corners of the valves; made all the joints in the pipes dead opposite to each other by filing and fitting them until they were right. I had a lot of work doing this, because the design of these engines being for open ports there is not much clearance about the passages.

The next thing I looked to was the lift of the inlet valves; I found that, with Messrs. Prestwich's setting, they only opened 11-64 in. This was quite sufficient when the auxiliary ports were open, but not enough with them closed. By adjusting the tappets I managed to get all my inlets a full 3-16 in. lift, but to do this I had to leave a clearance of only 6-1,000 in. between the tappet and the valve stem at the highest point on the back of the cam.

Exhaust valves and exhaust valve guides I treated in the same way, and left exactly the same clearance between the tappet and the valve stem.

I do not think the engine ought to run at a lower speed than 1,600 revolutions per minute if best results are desired. A valve lift of 3-16 in. is, in my opinion, not quite sufficient for this speed, and I decided on having the cam shaft taken out and enough ground off the back of the cam to allow the valves to lift about ¼ in. This can easily be done, but I had not time.

The setting of the valves on my engine when it came from Prestwich's was as follows :-
Inlet valves lifting approximately 1/8 in. down induction stroke and closing about 3/8 in. up compression stroke.
Exhaust valves lifting approximately 3-16 in. after the auxiliary ports had been uncovered, and closing over dead centre at end of exhaust stroke.

I advanced the timing one tooth, which in conjunction with the adjustments I had made to the tappets, made the timing just right. The inlet valves then opened on dead centre and closed about ¼ in. up compression stroke. The exhaust valves opened when the pistons were a full ½ in. from the end of exhaust stroke. A tooth either way in the timing makes practically no difference when the auxiliary ports are open, but it makes a great difference to the cool running and efficiency when the ports are closed.

From the first I never liked the carburettor as fitted to the engine, and in its place I fitted a No 40 White and Poppe. I fitted this below the crank case, so that I would have no trouble with pressure feed, and would, at the same time, reduce the danger of fire to a minimum. I connected a good large sized inlet pipe with very easy bends from the carburettor to the existing crown piece above, and have not the slightest hesitation in saying that the fitting of this carburettor played a very important part in the great improvement made to the engine. I consider the White and Poppe, if properly set, to be the best carburettor in the world for aeroplane work.

I know many have had these carburettors fitted to their engines and that they did not get wonderful results from them, but I feel quite certain that the carburettors were not rightly adjusted to the engine, or perfect results would have been obtained. I may say in connection with this, that I experimented to find if I could not do without a hot-air pipe, and I found that it was essential to fit one. I fitted a pipe 8 ins. long over one of my exhaust pipes and adjusted the carburettor to give best results when the engine had warmed up. Since then I have not had the slightest trouble with the engine, nor have I had to clean a sparking plug all the season, owing to the fact that I have got my mixture right at all positions of the throttle.

After making the above alterations I tested the engine for pull, and found that with one of T. W. Clarke's propellers, which gave 260 lbs pull before, it now gave a little over 320 lbs pull. There could have been no mistake about this increase in power, as I made the tests under exactly similar conditions, and, besides, the fact that the machine will now fly with a big passenger, while it would hardly fly before with the pilot alone, shows the wonderful improvement that has been made so far as power is concerned.

After the power test I tested for over-heating. Formerly, after running for five minutes the pull fell off very considerably. After alterations I ran the engine all out for twelve minutes without running any oil into it, and just allowing it to lubricate by splash from the crank-case. There were no signs of heating up whatsoever nor fall off in pull, and when I removed some of the auxiliary port plugs to see how the pistons were oiled I found they were all perfectly lubricated, whereas formerly they would have been quite dry'.

Harry sums up as stated in the main text and then completes his article as follows:

'Taking things all round, I am now very proud of my JAP engine, and, so far as re-liability is concerned, I could wish for nothing better. I have not cleaned a cyl-inder, ground a valve, nor made any adjustments whatsoever since last July, and the engine is pulling as well at the present moment as it was then'.

Appendix 12: Recent aerial view of the Growell farm-house showing the Long Field from which Harry flew in 1911. Lough Aghery is seen in the background.

Appendix 13: Map showing Harry's base established at Miskelly's farm, showing the proximity of the beach and Comber Road.

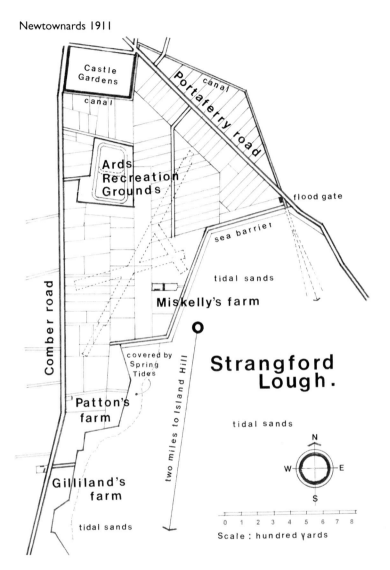

Newtownards 1911

154

Appendix 14: Extracts from RFC Communique No. 16: Combats in the Air, October 26th 1915.

'Lieutenant Williams and Lieutenant Hallam, No 10 Squadron in a B.E.2c when doing photography near Lille were attacked by a Fokker with deflector propellor at about 7,000 feet.

While manipulating the gun, Lieutenant Hallam was hit in the hand which prevented him from again using this weapon. A certain amount of manoeuvring then took place after which the pilot was hit in the arm and shoulder and lost consciousness.

The B.E.2c then started spinning, and Lieutenant Hallam seeing that the pilot was hit, climbed over between the two back struts and caught hold of the control lever. He moved this about, but nothing happened. He then tried to close the throttle. This did no good, the wire apparently having been broken. He then turned off the petrol, and getting the machine under control managed to land it just behind the French reserve trenches in square M.25 Sheet 36. The machine turned over, and Lieutenant Williams was thrown out. Lt. Hallam climbed out and assisted Lt. Williams who had lost a lot of blood. Eventually they were assisted and Lt. Williams' wounds attended to by men of the French Red Cross'.

Drawing 1: Mark I – Hillsborough, November 1909

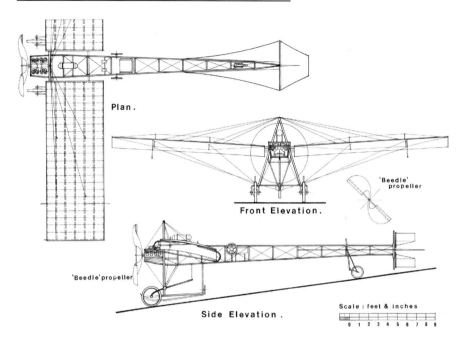

Plan.

Front Elevation.

'Beedle' propeller

'Beedle' propeller

Side Elevation.

Scale : feet & inches
0 1 2 3 4 5 6 7 8 9

Drawing 2: Mark IA – Hillsborough, December 1909

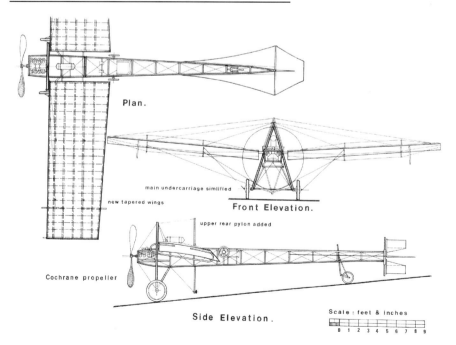

Plan.

main undercarriage simlified

new tapered wings

Front Elevation.

upper rear pylon added

Cochrane propeller

Side Elevation.

Scale : feet & inches
0 1 2 3 4 5 6 7 8 9

Drawing 3: Mark IC – Masserene, April 1910 (Mark IB similar in design, but without the extended ridge)

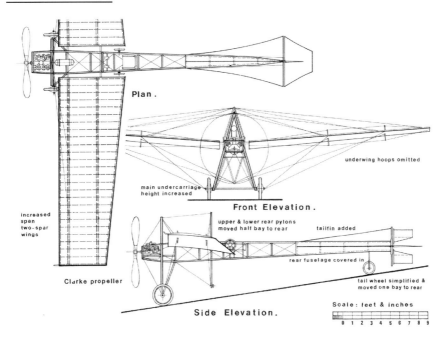

Plan.

underwing hoops omitted

main undercarriage
height increased

Front Elevation.

increased
span
two-spar
wings

upper & lower rear pylons
moved half bay to rear   tailfin added

rear fuselage covered in

Clarke propeller

tail wheel simplified &
moved one bay to rear

Scale: feet & inches

0 1 2 3 4 5 6 7 8 9

Side Elevation.

Drawing 4: Mark ID – Magilligan, June 1910 and Newcastle, July 1910

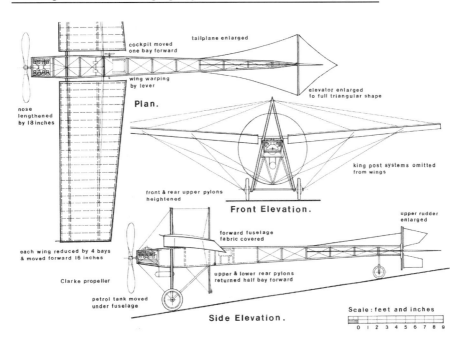

tailplane enlarged

cockpit moved
one bay forward

Plan.

wing warping
by lever

elevator enlarged
to full triangular shape

nose
lengthened
by 18 inches

king post systems omitted
from wings

front & rear upper pylons
heightened

Front Elevation.

upper rudder
enlarged

forward fuselage
fabric covered

each wing reduced by 4 bays
& moved forward 16 inches

upper & lower rear pylons
returned half bay forward

Clarke propeller

petrol tank moved
under fuselage

Side Elevation.

Scale: feet and inches

0 1 2 3 4 5 6 7 8 9

Drawing 5: Mark 1E – Magilligan Aug-Oct 1910

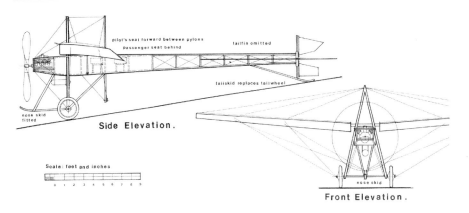

pilot's seat forward between pylons
Passenger seat behind
tailfin omitted

tailskid replaces tailwheel

nose skid
fitted

Side Elevation.

Scale: feet and inches

0 1 2 3 4 5 6 7 8 9

nose skid

Front Elevation.

Drawing 6: Mark 1F – Magilligan, Summer 1910 (experimental)

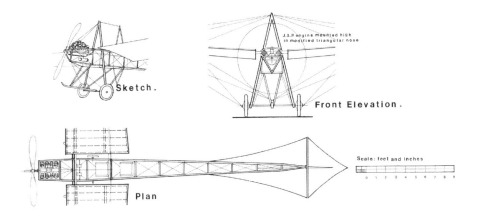

Sketch.

J.A.P. engine mounted high
in modified triangular nose

Front Elevation.

Plan

Scale: feet and inches

0 1 2 3 4 5 6 7 8 9